The Girlfriends' Guide to Getting Your Groove Back

"With an engaging mix of humor, firsthand experience, and the insights of other girlfriends, she urges women to relish this phase of motherhood (and their independence from diaper bags), while also realizing that they can't turn the clock back." —*Publishers Weekly*

The Girlfriends' Guide to Toddlers

"Chatty, hilarious, informative, and wise . . . Iovine offers the kind of frank, sanity-saving advice you might get from a beloved best friend who's already been there." —*Bookpage*

"Iovine and the Girlfriends are back at it again, granting us the benefit of their considerable experience on everything toddlerish." —*The Austin Chronicle*

"Well-written and graced with humor, *The Girlfriends' Guide* will, like a good friend, help get you through those first wobbly years of motherhood." —*Chicago Tribune*

"Iovine offers entertaining anecdotes and sage advice on raising kids from ages one to three . . . this seasoned mom knowledgeably walks readers through the toddler trenches . . . fans will be delighted in this latest volume in the *Girlfriends'* series, and new mothers warily approaching their child's toddlerhood will find that Iovine's take on these challenging years is as reasonable as that of any 'expert'—and quite a bit funnier." —*Publishers Weekly*

continued on next page . . .

The Girlfriends' Guide to Surviving the First Year of Motherhood

"Humor, honesty, and sisterly advice . . . a first-time mom's must-have guide."
—*USA Today*

"Invaluable . . . [a] funny, honest new volume." —*L.A. Parent*

"If humor is the best medicine, Vicki Iovine has all the tonic a new mother should need. Her information comes from experience and her humor from the heart. An invaluable dialogue with a girlfriend who's been there. And got the most from her adventure."
—*Rocky Mountain News*

The Girlfriends' Guide to Pregnancy

"A chatty, candid, laugh-out-loud primer for unseasoned moms-to-be." —*People*

"Iovine and her gaggle of Girlfriends are ready with reassuring and frequently irreverent advice." —*Newsweek*

The Girlfriends' Guide to Baby Gear

What to buy, what to borrow, and what to blow off!

Vicki Iovine

with Peg Rosen

A Perigee Book

Some of the Girlfriends' names have been changed to protect their privacy . . .
but Girlfriends, you know who you are.

"Keep Your Baby Safe: The Right Way to Install a Car Seat" reprinted by permission
of Weider Publications, Inc. Copyright © April/May 2002.

A Perigee Book
Published by The Berkley Publishing Group
A division of Penguin Putnam Inc.
375 Hudson Street
New York, New York 10014

First edition: January 2003

Visit our website at www.penguinputnam.com

Library of Congress Cataloging-in-Publication Data

Iovine, Vicki.
The girlfriends' guide to baby gear / Vicki Iovine with Peg Rosen.
        p.   cm.
Includes index.
ISBN 0-399-52845-8
1. Infants—Care.   2. Infants' supplies.   3. Consumer education.   I. Rosen, Peg.
II. Title.

RJ61 .I668   2003
649'.122—dc21
2002030366

Printed in the United States of America

10   9   8   7   6   5   4   3   2

Make new friends, but keep the old. One is silver and the other gold. To all my friends, my true wealth. Sorry, but you're all beginning to look a little gold around the edges to me.

—Vicki Iovine

Contents

Contents

Contents

Acknowledgments

Finally. The work, late nights, whining, nit-picking, obsessing, heated debate, and nervous laughter are over, and here is the end result. An honest-to-goodness book. Really and truly, it has been a collaborative effort and there are many thanks to give.

Vicki Iovine, thank you for your friendship through these many years and for the opportunities you have sent my way. You are a Girlfriend with a capital G and one heck of an inspiration. Thanks, Christine Pepe, for your encouragement and tolerance. You're not only a terrific editor but a great therapist.

Thanks go to the many professionals who came to the plate when I asked them to help with this book. Key among them are Claire Lerner, L.C.S.W., Child Development Specialist, Zero to Three; Jerrod Milton, R.Ph., director of Pharmacy Services, The Children's Hospital, Denver; Lyn Stevenson, R.D., The Children's Hospital, Denver; S. Honor Fullerton, M.D., Menlo Dermatology Medical Group, Clinical Assistant Professor of

Dermatology, Stanford University School of Medicine; Ed Mahon, Lakeland Baby & Teen Furniture; Laura Reno at the SIDS Alliance; Glenn Boonstra, DaimlerChrysler Fit for a Kid instructor and director of service, Borough Jeep, Wayne, New Jersey; Patti Di Filippo, certified child passenger safety instructor; and Sandy Waak, certified emergency nurse and certified child passenger safety instructor.

Then, of course, there are the Girlfriends whose experiences and advice are at the heart of this book. Bianca Bator, Judy Sciarra, and Jamie Scurletis—I love you and owe you big time for fielding all those late-night and early-morning interrogations about virtually every aspect of your maternal existence. Thanks also to Zori Levine, Georgia Scurletis, Gail Belsky, Kate Kelly, Jeannie Rosen, Julie Rosen, and Connie Fowler for your willingness to play along. As for the dozens and dozens of other Girlfriends who have participated in my Motherhood Network over the past years, I am indebted to you for sharing your stories, your wisdom, and your time. You all serve as a constant reminder of how the bond of motherhood really can bring people from all walks of life together.

Thanks to my mother and dad, Carol and Bob Rosen, for showing me firsthand how much fun childhood and parenthood can be. A huge thanks, as well, to Florence Freundlich. If someone had told me that my mother-in-law would turn out to be one of my very best Girlfriends, I'd have said they were crazy. Consider it—and the fact that this job got done—proof that anything is possible. Gabi—this has been one crazy year. Thanks so much for hanging in there and keeping everyone happy. We'll miss you.

Finally, thank you, thank you to the three most important individuals in my life. They are not Girlfriends. They are, in fact,

100 percent male. My dear husband, Paul, and my sons, Ben and Noah. You guys are my heart, my breath, the very meaning of my life. I love you "to the moon and back."

–P. R.

Why We Wrote This Book

I sincerely love how sweetly *The Girlfriends' Guide to Pregnancy* and *The Girlfriends' Guide to Surviving the First Year of Motherhood* have been embraced by new mommies and moms-to-be. I honestly never thought the reading group would ever expand beyond the Girlfriends who were mentioned by name and our close circle of friends. Early on, while I was noticing the first murmurings that complete strangers were reading my books and actually finding them useful, I met Peg Rosen. She was a senior editor at *Child* magazine and on her way to birthing the second of her two sons. At the time, in one of those wondrously fortuitous things, she became the editor of the column I've written for *Child* for the last five or six years (it all gets blurry after a while). She used to send me page notes like "Can't this be funnier?" or "Add that Vicki thing you do," and we spent many hours talking coast to coast about everything. I was in awe of her cosmopolitan outlook on parenting.

The other brilliant thing about Peg was that she was the de facto honcho of all product and merchandise information for *Child*. If it was for sale in any baby section, Peg had seen it, pulled it apart, poked the eyes out, and tried to sterilize it. I was so happy to learn that such a font of knowledge shared my sincere commitment to ending car seat misuse, preventing dog bites to toddlers' faces, and reducing most if not all accidents around swimming pools. Call us hysterical, call us intense, but CALL US if you want two great allies in protecting your precious children and making the entire family more at ease in this gigantic new responsibility called Parenthood.

This book is exactly what Peg and I searched for high and low when we were shopping to equip our first precious offspring. It's honest, it's not influenced by any corporate sponsorship, and it's the product of the Girlfriends' invaluable tried-and-true experience. We call it as we see it, and if it's too close to call, we give you several choices. Just pull out your pen and start marking away; the lists are all here for you. And just in case you're a little worried that such a nuts-and-bolts book might economize on the famous *Girlfriends' Guide* humor, relax, Mommy! We're still the same trash talkers we've always been.

Stay in touch! A book like *The Girlfriends' Guide to Baby Gear* is only as good as your feedback. Now, ready, set, CHARGE!

Top Ten Reasons Why
We Spend Too Much on Baby Stuff

10. Nothing looks good on us at this point, so who else is there to shop for?

9. You still can't believe this huge weight gain is going to result in a baby, so you accumulate physical evidence.

8. No self-respecting daddy would begrude money spent on a shopping spree for his own offspring.

7. An unspoken conviction that any gaps in our ability as mothers will be covered by acquiring the best baby equipment available, even if we have to take space in a storage unit to hold all the stuff.

6. Boredom, pure and simple. By the end of pregnancy, food gives us gas, fluids freak out our puny bladders, and sex, well, who even remembers what that is? The only thing more moving than a Braxton-Hicks is the rush of retail.

5. We believe that our children will need everything mentioned in the layette lists within the first hour of their birth. They will wear all five undershirts, three sleep sacks, and four seasonal hats simultaneously, while we will be sterilizing all their bottles, nipples, and rings, babyproofing the kitchen,

and reading the *Pat the Bunny* series, all on that first day of
life, and we don't want to be caught unprepared.

4. Our parents send us money for this express purpose, so
    we're just being cooperative kids.

3. If it doesn't already look like the baby has been living in the
    house for the last decade, people might think we're in denial
    about his arrival.

2. Anything, even a nail clipper, is absolutely irresistibly
    adorable in miniature. Air Jordans that are three inches long
    are unbearably precious, and a tiny pair of Osh Kosh B'Gosh
    overalls no longer than your forearm are good enough to
    eat. Don't get me started with the tiny sunglasses, biker jack-
    ets, or ballerina outfits.

1. We've finally been accepted into the secret cabal of women
    who know what breast shells are for and who consider A&D
    Ointment as essential as undereye concealer. We've waited
    for this all our lives, and by golly, we're going to get our
    money's worth out of the experience.

The
Girlfriends' Guide
to Baby Gear

Introduction, Or: The Strangest Shopping Spree of Your Life

Rev up your Visa card, Girlfriend. As a mommy-to-be, you will soon embark on what will be if not the biggest, then the most surprising shopping spree of your life. Far from your favorite houses of style, you will venture into a realm of retail that, as an adult, you may never have before considered. We're talking about fluorescent-lit stores with giraffes as their mascots, where tiny people run roughshod through the aisles. We're talking about obscure on-line boutiques peddling breast pumps and nipple shields.

What's surprising is how willingly you will surrender to this seismic change in orientation. Suddenly (round about the fifth or sixth month when nothing close to your prepregnant dress size fits), it will dawn on you that you will not be pregnant forever. That, indeed, a baby will come out of this whole zany escapade, and you must be equipped to care for it. Faster than you can say "Braxton-Hicks," you will find yourself examining rectal thermometers and diaper bags alongside other women with similarly burgeoning bellies. And you will do it with unimaginable passion.

You might, in fact, already be in acquisition mode. If this is the case, the Girlfriends are guessing that you are more than a little overwhelmed. A mommy-to-be must not only develop an entirely new shopping vocabulary (can you say Baby Björn?), she must determine what her and her baby's needs will be before that precious bundle even arrives.

To top it all off, every purchase, whether it's for a stroller or a pacifier, is fraught with anxiety because each item will come into contact with a precious new baby. And since most of us know deep down inside that *we have no business being entrusted with a vulnerable little life*, we become convinced that half the battle will be won by surrounding our angels with only the finest and most beautiful objects in existence.

The excitement, the anticipation, and yes, the fear of it all are absolutely palpable. Veteran mommy Girlfriends can sense it when we spot our soon-to-be sorority sisters waddling toward the bassinets at Baby Depot. So can the people whose job it is to arm you with all the "necessities" of new parenthood. Many of these folks and their intimate knowledge of all things baby are worth their weight in gold. But the fact remains that these mortals must make a living. And they don't generally do so by telling you that you should blow off that bottle warmer and spend the money instead on some extra hours of baby-sitting help.

That's What the Girlfriends Are For

As moms who have been around the block—once, twice, four or six times—we've not only shopped for baby gear, we've used it. Over and over again. Or barely at all. We can tell you how much you'll really use the pricey quilt that matches your baby bedding. And how happy you and your pudendum will be to come home from the hospital to that ungainly glider chair. We know that all those pristine outfits and gossamer-soft blankets will soon be spotted with poop, spit-up, and every other bodily fluid, and you'll ultimately be most interested in which one hides stains best and provides the easiest diaper access.

Now calm down. We're not about to ruin the romance of new parenthood or brag about how we've been able to tough it out with just a leather sling and a few swatches of hemp. We're aware that our ancient predecessors made do without baby wipes and vibrating bouncy seats, but no one has ever said they had a whole lot of fun doing so. We also realize that a new mom's comfort level is far different from a veteran's, and that erring on the side of overkill (like purchasing that bottle sterilizer) may be worth the expense if it buoys your confidence.

Our intention is to save you time, money, and brain cells by giving you something you won't find anywhere else: the Girlfriends' opinion. We are going to take you by the hand, walk you through every step of this whole baby-prep process, and give you our notes from the mothering trenches. We'll tell you straight out what you and your baby will need to stay safe and comfortable and what you will survive perfectly well without. We know where you can get away with cutting corners and when it's worth paying top dollar. We'll tip you off on products. But we're not going to get *too specific*, since manufacturers change models as often as professional hockey players do, and you'll go bonkers scouring store shelves for something that may no longer exist. Instead, we'll pinpoint features we think are important and— when we are so inclined—provide the names of one or two brands that are likely to carry what you'll want.

The Girlfriends are also going to make sure that you, your

partner (if you have one), and your household are equipped for the escapade ahead. 'Cuz just in case no one's told you this already, having a baby will affect just about every aspect of life as you know it. You will shower differently, you will cook differently, you will dress differently, you will travel differently, you will *exist* differently. We'll let you know about some of the less obvious shopping that should be done to prepare yourself.

Our final intention is to drill this point into your head: There may be gazillions of things you can buy to help care for and protect your baby, but none of them (except a car seat) holds a candle to what you can do with your own head, hands, and heart. Take our word for it: When your baby is born, you will be reborn. And the mother that emerges will surprise and amaze you. You are the one who will be your child's first and most important defense, and you will do a magnificent job of fulfilling that role. Whether you're armed with that $40 bottle sterilizer or not.

What We're Not Here To Do

Just like the Girlfriends have never claimed to be a substitute for medical advice, we do not claim to be the last word in product safety. We have not dropped high chairs from fifty feet up to see how they endured the wear and tear. We haven't blowtorched bottles to determine at exactly which point they liquify (at least not on purpose). We've got kids to take care of, remember? We happily leave those antics to the guys in the white lab coats at *Consumer Reports* or wherever else they may be doing that sort of thing (see the sidebar from our Girlfriend Pam the Safety Zealot). We urge Girlfriends to keep on top of product recalls and find out as much as they can about product safety ratings and guidelines. We will provide you with a list of sources for this important information. Read it and use it—because when you get down to brass tacks, keeping our babies safe is what matters most of all.

We are also not going to attempt to please every mommy-to-be out there. Our take on motherhood is shamelessly practical. Having a few kids and an attic brimming with old equipment has that effect on most Girlfriends. However, if you have the space in your home and the money to buy every piece of high-end baby paraphernalia imaginable, all power to you. But you may not really need our opinions. Simply march into your nearest baby store and give your salesperson carte blanche to gear you up with the best of everything. He'll be more than happy to help you and his child might even write you a thank-you note for financing his dream trip to Disney World.

From Pam the Safety Zealot, A Note About Product Safety:

As you cruise the baby-gear aisles of your local superstore or page through the baby product catalogs, it's easy to assume that what you see for sale is safe to use. This is the U.S. of A., isn't it? The land where a Styrofoam coffee cup must have a label telling you its contents are hot. Our government wouldn't allow things to be sold if they put a vulnerable little baby's life in danger! Right?

Well, it's not that simple. Save for a few exceptions (like car seats and cribs—and even those aren't customarily government-tested until after they hit the market), Uncle Sam generally leaves it up to baby-gear manufacturers to test their own stuff and determine if they've met preset (and often quite limited) government and industry standards. Even the industry's trade group, the Juvenile Products Manufacturers Association, does not require its own members to earn its official seal of approval, which mandates third-party safety tests.

In the vast majority of cases, this crazy system works pretty well. Big-name baby-gear companies are pretty darned conscientious because they have built their reputation by providing parents and their children with safe equipment they can depend on. (They also know how expensive lawsuits can be.) But you don't have to be Ralph Nader to figure out that this still leaves open a significant window for trouble. Just check out the recall lists on the Consumer Product Safety Commission Web site (www.cpsc.gov). Baby products and toys are well represented, to say the least.

Making matters worse is the fact that baby-gear companies feel they must churn out new and improved mousetraps every year in order to rack up revenue. Admittedly, this can, and does, lead to Eureka-esque innovations, like premoistened baby wipes. On occasion, however, this pressure to constantly reinvent leads to shoddy designs and insufficient testing. Products sometimes go off to the stores anyway. The tragedy is that, in the majority of cases, government safety agencies only get involved once a problem is reported. And that "problem" could be the injury or death of a baby.

For this reason, the Girlfriends take a conservative approach to the ever more complicated task of buying for your baby. Here's our prescription:

Don't go for the latest and greatest. Just like you might stay away from a new model car the first year it rolls off the assembly line, we think it's generally a good idea to steer away from spanking-new product designs when you are shopping for major gear. We're not talking about mere tweaks—like a change of fabric or the addition of a new toy on a bouncy seat. That is almost unavoidable since, as we said, manufacturers diddle with their product designs practically every year. We're also not talking about changes that are made to meet new safety standards. We mean that if XYZ Baby Company comes out with a new infant tub that's equipped with its own water heater or if ABC Infant, Inc., decides to start making car seats for the very first time, you should probably pass. Buy a product with a good track record, and if the latest and greatest performs without a hitch once on the market, you can tell your little sister about it.

Stay away from knockoffs and no-name products. We love a bargain as much as the next gal. But if an item is too cheap to believe or no one you know has ever heard of the brand you're considering, skip it. Obscure companies may not be as rigorous about testing their products as their more established competitors. They may also be difficult to reach—or altogether out of business—if you have a problem with their product or require customer service. THIS IS A RULE OF THUMB THROUGHOUT THE BOOK.

Keep track of recalls. You may have ignored recalls and warnings in your salad days. Consider it one of your new parental responsibilities. An easy way to do it: Log onto the CPSC's site (*www.cpsc.gov*) and subscribe to their recall subscription list. Specify that you want to know about product recalls that involve children, and they will automatically send you e-mail alerts if anything comes up.

Create a Paper Trail. As soon as you decide you're going to keep what you've bought, mail in that information/warranty

card that comes in the box. This is extremely important
because it will allow the manufacturer to get in touch with you
should there be a product recall. Keep all information pertain-
ing to your purchases in an easily accessible file.

Where to Get What You'll Need

Specialty retailers:

The old guard of the baby-gear world, these places are often inde-
pendently owned and are generally billed as "Baby and Youth Furniture" stores. (USA Baby is one of the larger independent chains,
with dozens of locations scattered around the country.) Inside
baby specialty stores, you'll find lots of better-name cribs, high
chairs, strollers, bedding, and layette wear; "deluxe" versions of
mass-market items like activity gyms and bouncy seats; and more
esoteric things—like the My Brest Friend nursing pillow—that
aren't widely sold at the big chains. You'll also encounter salespeople who have probably been in the business since you yourself
were in diapers, or at least high school. The upside here is that
these individuals tend to really know their stuff and can answer
just about any question you toss out at them. The owners also
quite often have the luxury of handpicking an inventory that they
feel good about and that meets the needs of their particular client
base. The downside is that these folks can use their knowledge to
convince you to buy "the best" of just about everything. You will
probably want to do some, but not all, of your shopping here.

Baby superstores:

Can you say "Babies 'Я' Us"? This huge offshoot of Toys 'Я' Us—plus smaller chains of its ilk, like Burlington Coat Factory's Baby Depot—has made life difficult for the specialty retailers but a whole lot easier for expectant and new parents. For the mass-market basics and a decent representation of specialty products, the superstores are about as close to one-stop shopping as you can get. Don't count on major insights from the salespeople, though. While you may occasionally find an experienced individual on the floor, on average, these folks generally seem almost as new to this game as first-time moms are.

Froufrou boutiques:

These stores are what may have convinced you to have babies in the first place. They are usually in the heart of a nice neighborhood and sport names like Baby Angel or Silver Spoon. Moses baskets brimming with blush-pink booties and plush stuffed bunnies line the walls. The racks are artfully laden with tiny $90 hand-knit cardigans, velveteen special-occasion coats, and lavish layettewear that is so soft, so gorgeously patterned it seems positively edible. THIS IS WHERE SWINGING SINGLES AND GREAT-AUNTS BUY BABY GIFTS AND WHERE MOMMY GIRLFRIENDS RUN WHEN THEY HAVE TO BUY LAST-MINUTE HOLIDAY OUTFITS AND SHOWER PRESENTS. By all means, pop by and pick up the occasional confection. These are probably not the best places, however, to shop in bulk for tiny, fast-growing babies unless a store is holding an incredible sale or you can't figure out what to do with all your money. (Call us if you need suggestions.)

General merchandisers:

The Wal-Marts and Targets of this world offer a decent selection of basic stuff at fair prices. (Could we sound more excited?) The big drawback is that baby bouncers are competing with blenders and bird feeders for shelf space, so you won't find the widest array of brands and models. The Girlfriends have found that you can also expect to receive service from someone who knows as much about baby gear, or probably less, than they know about yard furniture. If you happen to run across exactly what you want in the color and style you dream of, go ahead and buy it. Later on, when you're buying certain items in bulk, like diapers, or when you need an inexpensive stroller to keep in the trunk of your car, these stores can be a godsend. But you don't need to make your decisions based on what the big general merchandisers have to offer. There's lots more to choose from out there.

Warehouse clubs:

Joining a warehouse club is a lot like buying a minivan. It's not chic, it smacks of middle-age pragmatism, but boy, does it make sense when you have kids. As far as we're concerned, if you live near one of these places and have ample storage space at home, stores like Costco, SAM's Club, and BJ's Wholesale Club should be your definitive source for baby supplies that you will go through like crazy. Not only because it will generally save you money, but because you can buy in bulk, stay well stocked, and avoid mad dashes to the store (which is an insane concept when you have an infant). If you buy nothing more than wipes, diapers, and formula from your warehouse club, it may be well worth the membership fee and occasional migraine.

On-line and catalogs:

If used carefully, the Internet can be an expectant and new mom's best friend. You can research products to your heart's content—user reviews on sites like Babycenter.com and Epinions.com are invaluable. You can also track down and buy virtually any item you'll ever dream you might need—without even fastening your nursing flaps. Of course, shopping convenience goes right out the window if you have to haul your purchases to the post office in order to return them. That's why we recommend that you not buy major items on-line unless you have checked them out in person somewhere else or if you absolutely cannot get what you need locally. Also don't forget about shipping charges: The extra cost might not end up making sense.

Register This

If you think that registering for baby gifts seems forward, or greedy, or tacky, get over it. As moms who have attended God knows how many baby showers where every other gift is a Snugli or a sweater . . . as Girlfriends who have spent countless hours trying to figure out what coworkers and acquaintances have and don't have, we can tell you that, from the givers' perspective, registering is not only smart, it's thoughtful. Add to this the fact that gifts can often be ordered off a registry without actually having to make a trip to the store—and we're tempted to get down on our knees and beg you to heed our words. Of course—this is all assuming that you are having your first baby. Registering for subsequent kids can seem a little weird, we have to admit.

Our needs aside, registering is one of the biggest favors a first-time mom can do for herself. You will get exactly what you want and need, and it will seriously cut down on the amount of returns you'll have to make. Our tips:

- **Register just once.** Breaking up your wish list among several different stores is bound to create confusion. Instead, sign on with a retailer that sells the bulk of what you want and need. Then, if there's a particular item that's not available there—say, the baby bedding you're craving—take care of it yourself or invite Mom (or a similarly inclined gift giver) on a little shopping trip.

- **Opt for a retailer that specializes in baby gear** (for example, a baby superstore or an independent baby specialty store, rather than a general retailer), if possible. You will have a wider selection to choose from and a more knowledgeable sales staff with which to work.

- **Make service and stock the priority.** It's thoughtful to keep price in mind, but bargain hunting definitely takes a backseat to service and selection when you register. Make sure the sales staff is willing to field questions, take phone orders, and fax your registry list to gift givers. Ask if the store will deliver and assemble larger items. If they do, what's the charge? Check out if you will be able to make returns/exchanges and if there is a time limit for doing so. (Actual refunds vs. store credit shouldn't be a deal breaker, since we promise you will have reason to shop there in the future.)

- **Don't risk registering with cyber retailers.** Yes, there are all kinds of retail options on the Internet. But—as we all know too well now—on-line businesses can vaporize overnight. And let's just say that efficient administration and service aren't their general strong point. This might not be such a big deal if you are purchasing a random item yourself—in terms of a registry, though, we think it's a recipe for a nightmare. That's why we urge you to be conservative and register with a retailer that has a real, honest-to-goodness sales staff that can sit down with you in a real honest-to-goodness building. Then you will know where to go whining if or when there is a problem.

- **Find a retailer that has reach.** Now that we've dissed the Internet, we will say that it's an added bonus if a brick-and-mortar retailer has an Internet store and Internet baby registry. This way you will enjoy having a concrete contact, and everyone else will be able to see what's on your wish list without even leaving their desks. This is particularly handy for folks who live out of your area. (Just ask friends and family to alert you if they see an item on your registry but buy it elsewhere. Then you'll know to take the item off your list.) An excellent example that hits all the bases: Babies 'Я' Us, a baby superstore chain that has numerous retail locations and operates a solid Web site and registry in conjunction with Amazon.com.

- **Be smart about shipping charges.** If you'd rather that your out-of-town friends spent their money on the gift instead of the "getting there," see if a retailer will "hold" gifts that have been ordered and call for you (or your lackey) to pick them up.

- **Research before you register.** By the time you march up to the registry desk and ask for help, you should know exactly what you want (or you should be pretty close to it). That's why you have this book. That's why you have Girlfriends. That's why you have spent lots of time wandering around the store asking questions. If the sales help mentions an item you haven't yet considered, think carefully. Putting extraneous things on the list will reduce the chances that you will get what you really need.

- **Register for what you ideally want.** If you can't decide whether you should settle on a basic item or go for a more expensive version that has features you really would like, register for the fancier one (as long as the price isn't so astronomical that no one would buy it). If you don't end up getting it off your registry, you can always buy the less expensive one yourself.

- **Don't register for absolutely everything.** Since there is no telling what people will and won't buy off your wish list (and when they'll do it, especially if you are not having a shower), take care of the absolute immediate essentials yourself. Or let those closest to you (your sister, your best Girlfriend, your mom) know what on your registry you'd love to count on them for. These immediate musts include basic layette items, health and hygiene paraphernalia, the first place baby will sleep, feeding equipment, diapering gear, and the car seat. You should also probably avoid registering for niggly things like baby detergent or nursing pads—anyone but the most pragmatic Girlfriend will probably feel like a heel bringing those to a shower.

- **Go for a wide range of prices.** Gift givers generally have an idea of what they want to spend. So include some items on both ends of the price spectrum and lots in the middle (between $35 and $75).

- **Keep future needs in mind.** In general, it's best not to buy products too far in advance of when you'll actually use them. Technology can change; your actual needs may be quite different than what you expected. It's a shame, though, not to take advantage of everyone's gift-giving spirit around the time of your baby's birth. One solution: Our wily Girlfriend Cynthia actually registered for a number of items she wouldn't immediately need—like a convertible car seat and a high chair—exchanged what she received for a store credit, and shopped for what she actually wanted when the time was right. Some stores may also allow you to indicate on your registry that for certain flagged items you would prefer to receive a gift certificate as opposed to the actual gift. Yeah, it's kinda pushy. But if you're comfortable with the idea, so are we.

- **Get the word out.** If someone will be throwing a shower for you, she can make a note about where you're registered right on the invitation. If you do not plan to have a shower, train your family and very best Girlfriends to utter the following words to everyone and anyone who asks what the expectant or new mom needs: "She's registered at XYZ Baby, and I know she would be thrilled to receive anything off her list. Here's the phone number and Web site."

- **Hold off on actually buying stuff yourself until after the shower.** If someone is throwing you a shower, she should do it at least six weeks before your due date. Not only will this allow you to be somewhat prepared if you should deliver a bit early, it will also give you enough time to dash out and buy the essentials you didn't get at your shower.

The Bottom Line On Secondhand Stuff

The Girlfriends not only think it's okay to borrow, inherit, or buy certain used baby stuff, we think it's a shame not to. If defending the family piggy bank isn't an issue for you (or if asking for a handout feels funny), think of how you'll help the environment by reusing all those plastic contraptions. And how about all that closet space you'll be freeing up for those you love!

Before you run out to raid the attics of your nearest and dearest, however, you must promise us that you will heed what we are about to say: USED BABY EQUIPMENT, WHETHER IT COMES FROM YOUR SISTER OR A GARAGE SALE, CAN BE DANGEROUS. Older items may not meet current safety standards; wear and tear can compromise a piece's sturdiness or function. Babies have died as a result. The only way you should exercise the used baby stuff option is if you SWEAR TO US AND YOURSELF THAT YOU WILL NOT PUT YOUR BABY ANYWHERE NEAR A SECONDHAND PIECE OF GEAR UNLESS YOU HAVE DONE YOUR HOMEWORK. If you are not willing to stick to this rule, you should buy new. Period.

Don't roll your eyes. The Girlfriends don't often weigh in as the heavies, but this is one of a few areas where we don't fool around (we're also hard-asses about car seats which, by the way, should never be borrowed or purchased secondhand). Besides, the extra legwork isn't such a big deal. Here's the strategy:

FIRST, HUNT DOWN YOUR SOURCE: Your closest Girlfriends are a good place to start, since you'll have a good idea of what they have and how they treat their belongings. Unfortunately, chances are good that if you are having babies now, so are your contemporaries, and they'll need this stuff as much as you will. It's okay to cast your net wider. Chat up coworkers, your partner's coworkers, cousins, church acquaintances, yoga classmates, etc. If you're too shy to ask flat out, beat around the bush a little. Ask a mom of a young brood how she liked the stroller she used or where she bought her diaper bag. Dollars to doughnuts that at least one Girlfriendly soul—even if she barely knows you—will lunge for your arm and simply demand that you come by her house and help yourself to her baby booty. (And do take her up on it—you really will be doing her a favor.)

REMEMBER THAT BORROWING IS A TEMPORARY SOLUTION. In contrast to all-out inherited stuff, loaners must eventually be returned (that's the theory, at least). If you have another child, you might end up buying this stuff yourself anyway. Then again, that might not be such a big deal, since a few years down the line, you might be in a better financial position to afford it, and you'll have a better idea of what you want and need.

CHOOSE CAREFULLY. This is a time for diplomacy and restraint. Somebody is helping you out here—you're not in the position to kick tires or fire off a lot of tough customer questions. You will have to know what to say when your benefactor waxes poetic about her rickety bassinet with the stained mattress and insists that you take it. (Stock response: "It's soooo adorable, but I think I've actually got that base covered.") Ask your hostess how she liked various items and inquire about how they work. While she's doing her demonstration, watch to see if the latches, wheels, and other moving parts function well. Do the legs look sturdy? Slightly soiled fabrics (like the sling of a bouncy seat) can generally be machine washed, but don't go for anything that's too groaty unless you're really hard up—you'll be amazed at how loath you'll be to put your pristine newborn in it when the time finally arrives. Take a few things you feel fairly certain you'll use, thank your benefactor profusely, and be on your way.

DO YOUR HOMEWORK. Here's the pain-in-the-neck part, but make sure you do it. With paper in hand, write down the brand and model name, as well as the serial/model number of any gear you've scored. (The latter bit of data is usually marked on a sticker or tag somewhere on the item. If you can't find this information, and the manufacturer can't help you determine what it is, you're best off passing on the item.) Next, call the Consumer Product Safety Commission's hotline (800-638-2772) or log on at *www.cpsc.gov.* By following the prompts, you will be able to see if the items in question have been recalled. If your benefactor doesn't have the instructions that came with a particular piece of gear that has moving parts or must be assembled, call the manufacturer (you'll find a customer service phone number on their Web site and, quite often, on the product itself) and ask them to send you a copy. There's usually no charge. While you've got them on the phone, check to make sure that the item in question meets current safety guidelines.

As far as clothing is concerned, you don't have to be such a stickler—just give things a once-over to make sure there are no loose buttons, strings, bows, or other doodads that could pose a choking or strangulation hazard. Any loose-fitting pajamas for babies over nine months of age should have a label saying they are made of flame-retardant fabric. Secondhand toys are okay for older toddlers, but check to see that they are in good repair and are devoid of any potential choking hazards. Skip any used plastic-type infant toy or teether altogether—it could be made with PVC, a plastic that major manufacturers have been generally phasing out, since studies revealed it may release chemical toxins when regularly sucked on or chewed.

KEEP A RECORD. Start a list of everything you borrow—we promise you won't remember who belongs to what when the time comes to return the stuff. If an item has been recalled, let your benefactor know and ask if she would like you to get rid of it. If you simply decide that you won't need what you've borrowed or inherited, return it promptly so she can share the wealth with someone else and simply say you received a new one as a gift.

CLEAN IT UP. Or better yet, have someone else clean up what you've scored. Toss any fabric pieces that are washable into the machine. (Pay attention as you take the stuff off so you'll know how to get it back on.) Our Girlfriend Brett swears that Borax (like 20 Mule Power) diluted in water does a wondrous job of brightening up plastic equipment and is not as caustic as detergents—a comforting point if you will be doing the scrubbing yourself. The recipe she uses: Fill an empty spray bottle three-quarters of the way full with warm water. Add three tablespoons of Borax and two tablespoons of liquid dish soap. Put spray top back on the bottle, shake it up, and go to town. Write the recipe in permanent ink on the bottle so you'll know what's inside and how to make refills.

BORROW/INHERIT WITH CARE

Baby bathtub

Clothing

Towels

Diaper covers

Outerwear

Bouncy seat

Changing table

Dresser

Glider

Nursing stool

Baby monitor

Baby hangers

Infant activity gym

Stationary exerciser

Books about
    breast-feeding

Nursing pillow

Unused disposable
    nursing pads

Mobile

Infant car seat cover-up
Stay-warm stroller bag
Bottle drying rack
Dry formula dispenser

Baby food mill
Diaper bag
Diaper supply caddy

BORROW/INHERIT WITH EXTRA CARE

Front carrier

Baby swing

Baby carriage/pram/stroller (ask if owner has bug netting and rain shield to go with it)

High chair: Safety guidelines have recently changed

Booster seat for feeding

Baby backpack

BORROW/WITH EXTREME CARE AND CAUTION

Bassinet (No family heirlooms, please. Make sure legs and mattress supports are sturdy.)

Crib bedding

Portable play yard (lots of recalls in this department)

BUY NEW

Nursing bras

Crib

Crib mattress

Car seat

Breast pump

Bottles and nipples

Infant toys and teethers (anything made of plastic that can be mouthed by a young baby)

Health and hygiene paraphernalia

Part 1

Buying for Baby

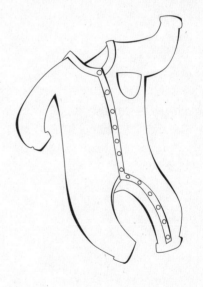

CHAPTER ONE

The Car Seat: The One Purchase Every Girlfriend Got Wrong

We know. You want to talk about the delicious stuff. Soft, tiny sweaters. Nursery furnishings. Baby buggies. And here we are talking right off the bat about car seats. *Thunk.* Car seats! Before you put this book down and use it as a pillow for a nice long nap, let us explain.

Learn from Our Mistakes, Not Your Own

When we started preparing for our babies' arrival, we knew—like you probably know—that we'd have to get a car seat. We knew, in fact, that the law wouldn't let us drive away from the hospital if our newborn wasn't strapped in to one of these devices. So we put "car seat" on our long to-do list, figured we'd ask our Girlfriends what they used when we had a chance, and got busy with other things.

Months later, with layette and nursery matters monopolizing our mind, it occurred to us that we still had to deal with that darned car seat. We poked around a bit, and frankly, in the midst of all the excitement, the issue didn't seem all that appealing. The clunky contraptions all sort of looked the same. Information on the subject was confusing, scary, and overwhelming. On a plate full of delectable goodies, procuring a car seat was the proverbial spinach.

Eventually we got the chore out of the way as painlessly as we could. Alessandra—who paid top dollar for just about everything from the finest Italian crib to the purest organic layettewear—borrowed a car seat from her sister-in-law. Lacey, who practically started weeping when she saw all the car seats she had to choose from at the superstore, asked the teenage clerk for his recommendation. By the ninth month of our first pregnancies, though the crib was up and the nursery was furnished, most of us had yet to take our car seat out of its box (or out of our friends' attics). Much as we hate to admit it, our car seats generally ended up getting installed by a relatively clueless husband or friend while we were eating Jell-O in the maternity ward.

Is it any surprise that our entire approach to the matter read like a laundry list of Car Seat Cardinal Sins? We found this out only after Pam the Safety Zealot took her car and car seat to something called a child seat safety inspection at a local car dealership. She came back trembling at the thought of how truly scary her—and all of our—mistakes and misjudgments had been. WE HAD LITERALLY PUT OUR BABIES' LIVES AT RISK. In some cases, for years.

We don't want you to make the same mistake. So if there's just one piece of information you can take away from this chapter, it should be this:

CAR SEATS ARE NOT JUST ANOTHER PIECE OF BABY EQUIPMENT. They may be sold in the same places as are strollers and stuffed animals. They may be made by the folks who bring you bouncy seats and baby backpacks. But car seats are very serious—often complex—pieces of gear. They are notoriously difficult to install correctly. Not all models are necessarily compatible with all cars. How you select yours, as well as how you use it, can save or endanger your baby's life. Get going early so you have the patience and perspective to get this complicated issue straight.

What You Need to Know

Now that we've gotten that off our chest—and thoroughly intimidated you—let us make you very happy and relieved. Realizing what a hairy issue this car seat thing is, we sent Pam the Safety Zealot to car-seat school. (There really is such a thing—folks spend days on end studying how to use and install car seats so they can help moms like us. Once they graduate, they are called child passenger safety technicians.) We let poor Pam watch all the hair-raising crash-test footage of car seats that weren't strapped in tightly. We let her struggle to install every imaginable car seat in every imaginable type of car. We made it her job to tease out the simplest and safest way to tackle the car-seat task. Here are Pam's car-seat crib notes for already overwhelmed parents-to-be.

The Basic Options:

There are two basic types of car seats that are appropriate for healthy newborns:

INFANT-ONLY SEATS: These are those little bucket seats with the handle that moms tote in and out of their car and snap onto strollers and grocery carts. Most can be attached to and removed from a plastic base that you fasten into your car. This type of seat faces to the rear of the car only. Most have an upper weight capacity of between 20 and 22 pounds and a maximum height capacity of 26 to 27 inches.

CONVERTIBLE SEATS: A convertible seat is bigger and bulkier and basically stays put in the car. It is designed so that it can face rearward for infants and toddlers and forward for older toddlers and preschoolers.

If you have a premature or very small infant, or one that has particular health issues, you may have to use a:

CAR BED: This is basically a restraint that keeps your infant in a horizontal position. Use this only if your physician tells you to do so.

The New Technology:

There are many reasons why car seats aren't easy to install correctly. Probably the biggest bugaboo is the fact that, until recently, you had to use a seat belt to hold your car seat in place. The concept sounds simple enough. But seat belts are actually very complex pieces of equipment. Getting them to effectively "lock" a car seat into position can require technical knowledge and elbow grease many parents don't have.

The good news is that as of September 2002, all new car seats sold in the United States had to be equipped with something called LATCH (Lower Anchors and Tethers for Children). It's a new, universal attachment system that does not require the use of seat belts at all. Since all vehicles and car seats will have the same corresponding attachment devices, it will simplify installation and lessen the chance for misuse. Here's how it works: In most cases, LATCH car seats have two small seat-belt-like straps that hook on to corresponding metal bars located in the rear crack of a vehicle's backseat. A top tether—a feature that was phased in earlier on—comes off the top of the car seat and attaches to a third fixed anchor in the vehicle. The top tether is only used with car seats when they are forward facing. (Britax brand car seats, which do use a top tether when they are rear facing, are currently the only exception to this rule.) LATCH isn't a cure-all, and it can still be a challenge to use correctly, but it's certainly an improvement over the old seat-belt method.

Being the smart Girlfriend you are, you've probably surmised what the catch is here: In order to use the LATCH features on a car seat, one must have a LATCH-equipped car. Not a problem if you have or are buying a late-model vehicle, since LATCH features have been required on most new automobiles sold in the United States since September 2002.

But what's a gal to do if her car ain't so fresh from the assembly line? Don't fret. Simply keep these points in mind:

- **LATCH car seats can still be installed the old-fashioned way.** If you don't have lower anchor points in your car (check your vehicle manual; some car models were equipped with them before the law formally went into effect), you'll just ignore the corresponding features on your car seat and strap it in with your vehicle's seat belt. Your baby will still be safe; proper installation will simply be a bit more difficult.

- **Top tether anchors can be added to most cars.** Unlike lower anchors, which really just ease installation, top tethers provide a direct safety advantage: They minimize head and neck injuries by reducing how far a child's head can thrust forward during a collision. (Again, unless your car-seat manual says otherwise, top tethers are only used when a car seat is in the forward-facing position.) If you have an older model car, it's worth having it retrofitted so you can take advantage of this safety feature. Your vehicle manual will tell you if and where a tether anchor can be installed. Ford, DaimlerChrysler, and GM retrofit many of their older vehicles free of charge. Most other dealers will do the job for a reasonable fee.

When to Use What

Start out with an infant seat.

In most cases, they provide a better fit for young babies than rear-facing convertible seats. The detachable baby carrier is also a huge convenience—you can tote it in and out of the car, snap it into a stroller (we'll tell you about that later), and use it as an extra baby seat in the house. (Just don't put the baby carrier on elevated surfaces like a table or bed. The floor is the safest spot to avoid injury as a result of falls.)

Next, move to a rear-facing convertible seat.

When your baby outgrows either the weight or height capacity of her infant seat, this will be your next step. Hold off on actually buying your convertible seat until your baby is a few months old—safety standards and technology are changing rapidly, and you'll want the most up-to-date model.

Do not rush to turn the convertible seat to face forward!

The most recent AAP recommendation is to keep babies rear facing until they are one year *AND* 20 pounds *AT THE ABSOLUTE BARE MINIMUM.* The longer your baby stays facing rear, the better support his vulnerable spinal cord will have in the event of a collision. So keep your child facing rear until he reaches the maximum rear-facing weight or height capacity of the seat. These days that's about thirty pounds or until his head is within an inch of the top of the seat (check your car-seat manual for specifics). NO CHILD UNDER ONE YEAR OF AGE SHOULD BE TURNED TO FACE FORWARD, REGARDLESS OF HIS WEIGHT OR HEIGHT.

Don't consider using seat belts alone until your child is about eight years old.

That's a long way off. But hey, we'll just plant that seed in your mind. After your "baby" outgrows his forward-facing convertible, you'll need to move him to a forward-facing car seat with a higher weight and height capacity or, if he's heavy enough, a belt-positioning booster. (See our recommended Web sites in this chapter for further details.)

Features to Look For

Infant-Only Car Seats

The following features will make it easier to use your infant-only car seat and secure your baby correctly:

A DETACHABLE BASE: Most infant-only car seats come with this feature nowadays. It allows you to install the base once, then simply snap the infant seat in and out of it. If you have more than one car, buy an extra base. Most brands sell them separately, and they are relatively inexpensive.

BUILT-IN ANGLE ADJUSTER: To keep an infant's head from flopping forward and possibly blocking his airway, a rear-facing car seat must be installed at the manufacturer's recommended angle, usually between 30 and 45 degrees. Adjustable bases have a foot that can be raised and lowered to help you reach the correct angle. Many seats now also have a gauge on the side that tells you if the angle is correct. The latter is helpful but not a must—if your car is parked at an angle, the gauge can be wrong. A simple way to eyeball it yourself: When the car-seat *base* is horizontal to the ground, the *seat* itself will be at the manufacturer's recommended angle for your child.

AN EASY-ADJUST HARNESS: The straps that come over your baby's shoulders and actually hold her in the car seat are called the harness. To do their job well, these straps must be snug against your baby's chest. Some car seats require you to pop out a metal bar in the back of the seat and rethread the harness when you want to adjust it. Avoid this if possible—it is time-consuming and may discourage you from making the harness tight enough. A better choice is an adjust mechanism which allows you to simply pull on a strap in order to tighten or loosen the harness. We're partial to the models that have this feature located on the front, as opposed to the back, of the seat.

A FIVE-POINT HARNESS: Once you put your baby into the car seat and place the harness over him, you must fasten him in. Some car seats have a "three-point" harness, which requires snapping just one buckle into a mechanism between your baby's legs. Some car seats have a five-point harness, which requires snapping two smaller pieces into a larger one. No question, the five-point harness is a bit trickier to use. But we—and many child passenger safety experts—believe it's worth the trouble since it allows the harness to fit a bit closer to your baby's body.

MULTIPLE-HEIGHT HARNESS SLOTS: If you look at a car seat, you will see that the harness straps feed out from slots located at the back of the car seat. When a child is rear facing, those harness slots should sit at or below his shoulders. If you have a small baby, this could be a problem if there is only one set of slots and his shoulders don't reach them. To cover your bases, seek out a seat that has at least two harness-height positions.

Convertible Seats

30-POUND (OR HIGHER) REAR-FACING CAPACITY: The longer your child sits rear facing, the safer he or she is.

FIVE-POINT HARNESS: Like the infant-only seat, a convertible's five-point harness provides the closest fit. When your child is forward facing, a five-point harness will also distribute crash forces most evenly over his body.

EASY-TO-ADJUST HARNESS AND TOP TETHER STRAPS: Look for mechanisms that can be cinched tighter with one hand, as opposed to being threaded and rethreaded.

What to Skip/What's Inconsequential

LUXURIOUS CUSHIONING AND PADDING: While it is of no harm and may look more comfy, this stuff has nothing to do with crash protection.

OVERHEAD SHIELDS: You've probably seen convertible car seats with this harness mechanism around—the seat looks like it has a big arm rest in front of the child. Overhead shields (also called tray shields) provide no safety advantage, are difficult to fit over larger toddlers, and may even pose a contact hazard during a collision if a child's head is thrown forward far enough. Overhead shields particularly shouldn't be used in the rear-facing position with a very young infant. The fit will not be close enough, and the child's face will not rise far enough above the shield. For similar reasons, the experts aren't so hot on T-shields, another shield-type of harness that has virtually been phased out at this point. Note: In certain situations, shield-style car seats may be appropriate. Case in point: Children who are transported to school or daycare in a bus or van may be put in a shield seat so the monitor or caregiver does not have to stick his or her hand between the child's legs. (An icky thought, but that's the world we live in.)

Can We Recommend Some Brands?

The official party line among CPS technicians is: There is no one safest car seat. The "best" car seat is a new car seat that fits your baby, your car, and your budget, and one that you will use correctly every time. Here's what techs say when they're on their coffee break: Darned straight there are some car seats that are easier to use and install correctly.

So you wanna know what some of those favorites are? The Girlfriends want to tell you. But remember—this is just a starting point. This doesn't mean there aren't other models that would suit your needs just fine. It doesn't mean what we're recommending won't be recalled or discontinued next week. It doesn't mean something better won't be out by the time this book is published. You'll still have to "try before you buy" to make sure our suggestion works for you. But here goes nothing:

Infant-Only Car Seats

GRACO: Graco makes one rear-facing infant-only seat. It is available with all the aforementioned features and is relatively easy to install tightly in most vehicles—whether they are equipped with LATCH or not. A simple squeeze mechanism makes the carrier a breeze to get out of its base, and an audible "click" lets you know it's locked back in securely. Since the weight limit is 20 pounds and the fit is snug, some babies grow out of this seat quickly. Not a big issue, but the child will need to be moved into a rear-facing convertible seat sooner. Extra bases, a big convenience if you have more than one vehicle, can be purchased separately.

Convertible Car Seats

BRITAX: Yes, Britax convertible car seats cost a bundle. We think they're well worth the price. They are a breeze to install in most any vehicle, whether it is LATCH-equipped or not. A tether that's used when the seat is in the rear-facing position generally makes it easier to achieve the manufacturer's recommended angle for young babies and also increases the seat's stability. Built-in lock-offs do away with the need for locking clips, those metal gizmos that must be used with certain types of seat belts found in older cars. Even the most basic Britax convertible is loaded with user-friendly features, like wide harness straps made from polyester, which don't twist up like the skinny, slippery nylon straps found on many other car seats. There are even little harness "holders" that keep the straps up and out of the way so you can avoid "digging" the harness straps out from under your baby once you put him in the seat. Also of note: The Britax has energy-absorbent foam in the upper torso and head area, in addition to standard foam that stretches from below the head to the bottom of the seat. Competitors generally only have energy-absorbent foam stretching from the top of where a child's head lies to the base of the neck. There's no public crash data to prove this makes the Britax safer, but common sense tells us it probably provides some extra protection.

GRACO: "A great basic seat" is how technicians consistently refer to Graco's affordable and easy-to-install ComfortSport convertible. It has a relatively narrow base, which encourages compatability with a wide array of vehicle seats, and a five-point harness that's easy to adjust. The seat's bottom harness slots are lower than some others', which provides a good fit for small babies when it is used in the rear-facing position.

A Big Fat Warning About Car-Seat Accessories

With a very few exceptions (which we'll tell you about), you should not use any item on your car seat that did not come with it or was not made specifically for it. Same goes for your vehicle seat and seat belts. The reason? Regardless of what a gizmo's packaging says, regardless of what "crash tests" they say they've done, the manufacturers of "after market" accessories are not in the position to prove that their products are effective or even safe to use on car seats and vehicle seat belts. The only parties that are currently qualified to make that determination are the car-seat and vehicle manufacturers themselves, or the National Highway Traffic Safety Administration. To date, they have not conducted crash tests with after-market products and have not endorsed their use.

What's Not Okay

- **Tightening devices.** These gadgets are intended to eliminate slack in the vehicle seat belt when you are using a non-LATCH car seat. Don't use them. If one of these were to detach during a collision, some experts believe it could become a dangerous projectile in the car and might introduce slack into the vehicle belt.

- **Car-seat toy bars.** The goal is to keep the area in front of your baby as free of potential contact hazards as possible.

- **Harness and seat padding.** This category includes those little cushions you can buy for the harness straps "to make baby more comfortable," as well as any separately purchased padding that goes under your baby's body or head. In the event of a collision, this material will become compressed and may allow what seemed like a snug harness to become too loose. The only exception: If such accessories come with the car seat, it means they have been crash-tested by the car-seat manufacturer and shown not to negatively affect the seat's performance.

- **Baby-minding mirrors.** These little mirrors usually attach to the back of the vehicle seat or the rear window above where your infant car seat is installed. In the event of a collision or short stop, one of these can easily detach, and your baby will probably be the first thing it hits. If you want to use a mirror of this type (which really isn't necessary and may even distract your attention from the road), make sure it is soft and very, very lightweight.

What Is Okay

- **Padding that surrounds baby.** Very young infants often need a little bit of extra support for their floppy necks and tiny bodies when they are sitting in a car seat. To solve this problem, CPS technicians very often roll up towels or receiving blankets and place them *alongside* the baby and *around* his head. There are also some products that accomplish the same thing. This is all okay. The key point here is that *nothing should be placed between your baby and the harness or the car seat itself.*

- **Infant car-seat cover-up (not to be confused with car-seat covers, which are basically slipcovers for car seats).** Cover-ups designed to go over infants sitting in rear-facing infant-only car seats provide an excellent way to keep infants warm in the colder months. They're convenient—you don't have to struggle with heavy coats and snowsuits. And they offer a safety advantage—less outerwear allows you to make the harness tight to your child, not to his winter coat (it's that excess padding thing again). Once you strap your baby in, you can even lay more blankets on top before popping the bubble on. Just be sure the "bubble" you buy fits *over and around* the outside of the seat, has a generous opening for baby's face, and does not interfere in any way with the harness. Noel Joanna, Inc. (NoJo) makes one that meets these specifications.

- **Towels and other soft bolsters for rear-facing seats.** In some cases—especially if a rear-facing seat does not have an adjustable base—it's necessary to put something under the seat base in order to achieve the manufacturer's recommended angle for rear-facing babies. It's okay to use a rolled-up towel, as some car seat manuals recommend. CPS techs also like to use—would you believe—short lengths of pool noodles, those long, spongy water toys. These tend to compress less than towels do—so you won't need to use as many—and you won't be tempted to pull them out from under the car seat if someone spits up or spills a milk shake in the car. If your vehicle seat is very slanted, you can bundle and duct-tape together up to three equal lengths of pool noodle and stick them under the car-seat base. *This technique should only be used with rear-facing car seats. In most cases, forward-facing car seats should be as upright as possible.*

Who You Can Trust for Info and Advice

Erroneous car-seat information is everywhere. We've heard salesclerks tell shoppers that most car seats are basically the same except for the fabric. Uninformed pediatricians have told a number of Girlfriends it was "okay" to face babies forward before their first birthday (a potentially deadly mistake, regardless of a child's weight). Product guides and catalogs often recommend accessories that safety experts clearly denounce. Heck, even a car salesman whose manufacturer is famous for putting safety first gave our Girlfriend Jenny some seriously scary advice about her car's built-in booster seat. (Just in case you're curious: It's never okay to tuck a vehicle shoulder belt under a child's arm in order to prevent it from riding up on his neck.) None of these mistakes is mean-spirited. Considering how complex the car-seat issue is and how fast it's changing, it's actually easy to understand how the issues can be misunderstood. That's why we want you to be very cautious and only accept advice from sources and individuals who are truly qualified to provide it.

These sources include (but are not limited to):

THE AMERICAN ACADEMY OF PEDIATRICS, *www.aap.org.*, 847/434-4000: While you shouldn't assume that individual doctors are up to snuff on the subject (they're up to their eyeballs in other important stuff, like insurance red tape), you can trust the car-seat info on the AAP's Web site. It's clear, it's thorough, and there's a full listing of all new car seats sold in the United States, along with their vital specs. You can also call the AAP for a free printed copy of this information.

THE NATIONAL SAFE KIDS CAMPAIGN: *www.safekids.org.* 800-441-1888; This child-safety advocacy group sponsors the training of many of the CPS technicians currently at work in the United States. Their Web site has helpful car-seat selection advice.

SAFETYBELTSAFE U.S.A: *www.carseat.org.* There's lots of up-to-date, accurate information on this vigilant advocacy group's Web site, plus a helpful on-line car seat "checkup" for those who might not have access to a real live CPS technician. You can also leave a message on their Safe Ride Helpline, 800-745-SAFE (800-747-SANO-Spanish), and someone will call back and verbally "walk" you through a car-seat checkup.

THE NATIONAL HIGHWAY TRAFFIC SAFETY ADMINISTRATION: *www.nhtsa.dot. gov,* 1-888-DASH-2-DOT. These are the government guys who regulate car seats and oversee child passenger safety. The Web site delivers just about all you need to know on the subject, including recalls, safety standard updates, and buying and usage guides.

CERTIFIED CHILD PASSENGER SAFETY TECHNICIANS: These individuals have met rigorous training requirements set by the National

Highway Traffic Safety Administration. Police officers, fire personnel, hospital staff, general do-gooders, and even some car-seat salespeople are among those who are being certified these days. CPS techs are not correct 100 percent of the time; if something they say sounds off base, check their information against one of the Web sites listed here. Also be sure to ask for an individual's credentials—and ideally an ID—before accepting any advice. You can find a CPS technician in your area on the NHTSA Web site, *www.nhtsa.dot.gov.* (You can trust our information because it has been provided by Pam, our CPS technician, and reviewed by some of the nation's top CPS instructors.)

What You Absolutely Must Know About Using Car Seats Correctly

Books and Web sites are brimming with articles and guides about how to actually install and use car seats. The problem is, there's so much information to absorb that people's eyes quickly glazeth over. Sometimes key points get buried in the morass. We'll leave the morass to the other guys. For the Girlfriends' condensed version of all you must absolutely know, see our appendix.

Why Used Car Seats Are Taboo.

Buying a car seat secondhand is a terrible idea because there is no way to be sure that it has not been in a crash. And a car seat that has been in a crash is no longer structurally sound enough for use. Even if you have the opportunity to borrow a seat from a Girlfriend with a perfect driving record, skip it. Older seats may not meet current safety standards, which are changing at a very rapid pace. Give your baby her best shot at having the best, most up-to-date protection and buy new. If you can't afford this expense, numerous charitable organizations give out car seats free of charge. Call the hospital where you are scheduled to deliver (start with the community service office; you might also try the maternity ward itself); they will probably be able to refer you to an appropriate car-seat source in your area. There may even be a car-seat donation program in the hospital itself.

The Fail-Safe, Anxiety-Free Approach to Buying and Installing a Car Seat

You know what Pam the Safety Zealot said after she spent four straight days studying to become a certified child passenger safety technician? IF THEY EXPECT PARENTS TO GET THIS CAR SEAT THING STRAIGHT ON THEIR OWN, THEY MIGHT AS WELL LET US PICK OUT AND INSTALL OUR OWN AIR BAGS, TOO. That's why we consider a car-seat checkup with a CPS technician absolutely vital. Consider it the "other" mandatory checkup to ensure your baby's well-being.

With that in mind, we urge you to take this approach to procuring and installing your baby's car seat:

1. **Locate a certified child passenger safety technician in your area and schedule an appointment.** Do this first since many technicians are booked up to two months in advance. The National Highway Traffic Safety Administration's Web site (*www.nhtsa.dot.gov*) offers a nationwide

directory of certified inspectors as well as a calendar of scheduled checkup events. If there isn't a CPS tech in your area, move to step three (don't worry, we're not leaving you high and dry).

2. **Pinpoint a few car-seat models that you'd like to try out.** We've listed some good basic candidates in this chapter. When you make that appointment for your car seat checkup, see if the CPS tech has a recommendation for your particular car. You might also want to log on to *www.carseatdata.org*, an unofficial technician-run site that keeps a list of car/car-seat compatabilities.

3. **Buy the top contender.** There are many different versions of some car seats. Make sure the one you buy has the features you want (see our box on important features). Hold on to the receipt.

4. **Bring it home and bring it out.** Don't just stash that car seat away somewhere. Take it out of the box and deal with it *tout de suite*.

5. **Read the car-seat directions.** It sounds obvious. But the fact is many parents turn to the car-seat manual as a last resort for troubleshooting, when it should be the very first thing they do. Don't just skim that dry, technical text—read it line by line, because it includes some not-so-obvious information about your specific car seat that can directly impact your child's safety.

6. **Read your vehicle manual.** Its car-seat section is a vital resource most parents completely overlook. If you do not have the manual for your car seat or vehicle, contact the manufacturer, and they will send one. *If you find your-*

self wondering at this point if it might be better to take your baby home by bicycle, you can skip Steps 6 and 7 and proceed directly to Step 8. You'll simply have to be extra sweet when you arrive at your car-seat checkup—especially if your car seat is still in its box.

7. **Now try installing the seat.** In each of your vehicles, if you have more than one. FOLLOW DIRECTIONS EXACTLY. For non-LATCH installation tips, see our appendix.

8. **Go inside, curse a little if you need to, and have a glass of water.** If your husband is doing this, he might need a Scotch or a sedative.

9. **Report for your car-seat checkup.** Allow a CPS tech to pat you on the back for your good work. Then let him or her fine-tune your car-seat installation and show you how to use your car seat properly.

10. **If you don't have a CPS tech nearby, call SafetyBeltSafe U.S.A.** If you leave a message on their Safe Ride Helpline, 800-745-SAFE (800-747-SANO-Spanish), someone will call back and verbally walk you through a car-seat checkup. Don't wait until you're in labor to call, however—it can take them a while to respond.

11. **If you don't own a car, buy one of the seats a CPS tech has recommended and hope for the best.** See if a friend can drive you home from the hospital (as opposed to taking a taxi), and try installing the base in her car a few weeks before you are due.

When to buy your car seat

We're willing to argue that an infant-car seat should be your first official baby purchase. (As long as the car you have is the one you will be driving after your baby arrives.) This will give you enough time to try installing the seat correctly yourself, to take it to a car-seat checkup with a certified passenger safety technician, and to go through the procedure all over again if it turns out that your initial purchase is incompatible with your car. By the beginning of your eighth month, the car seat (or at least the base) should be properly installed in your vehicle and ready to go. If you're superstitious or if doing this feels funny, hide it from sight with a blanket or towel. The last thing you want when you leave the hospital with your baby is to find your partner struggling to install the seat in the parking lot. It happens.

Where to buy a car seat

You can tackle this task at a number of places, ranging from wholesale clubs to discount chains to some specialty stores. Unless a store says it has salespeople that are CPS technicians (and these individuals have proof of certification) service shouldn't be a big factor here. (Since, as we said, erroneous information is absolutely rampant.) What matters is that the retailer you choose offers the models and brands you're interested in, competitive prices, and a generous return policy—you're going to take the seat home and try installing it in your vehicle(s) before committing to it. Since "try before you buy" is the M.O. with car seats, don't buy over the Internet unless you've tried out the exact model you see on-line in your car first to make sure it's compatible. (You might try installing a Girlfriend's seat.) With all this said, your best bet is probably the baby superstores.

CHAPTER TWO

The Layette,
Demystified,
Plus Other Baby
Wardrobe Wisdom

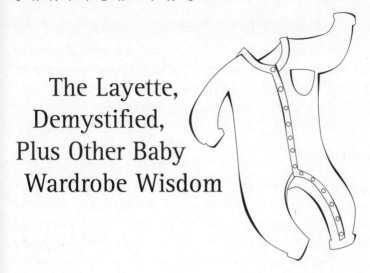

Now that we've bushwacked our way through some of the heavy-duty stuff, let's talk about the softer side of preparing for baby. Specifically, what that little cherub will wear during his first several months on this planet.

When to buy

You can go ahead and buy your essential layette pieces (we'll elaborate on the layette below) around your seventh month. If you're superstitious, have a Girlfriend keep the stuff at her house or ask the store if they'll hold it for you if you put down a deposit. Similarly, if you don't know if you're having a boy or a girl and want to avoid buying everything in yellow, see if the store will allow you to put down a deposit and have two different layettes set aside. When you give birth, a pal can simply swing by and pick up the appropriate set. Some stores actually have a "we deliver when you deliver" policy. As far as cute outfits and non-layette wear goes—don't bother buying this stuff in advance (unless it will markedly improve your mood at a given moment). It's prime fodder for gift givers and isn't an immediate necessity. You can always fill in holes after baby arrives.

Where to buy

Get your essentials from a store that has good, solid brands, great prices, and a generous return policy. We particularly love the Carter's outlet stores for layette wear—for all the above reasons and because they have all the basics you'll need. Baby play clothes (in addition to layettewear) can be found at any number of other places as well, from baby superstores to less obvious spots such as SYMS and other fashion discounters. Certainly check out specialty stores like Old Navy and babyGap. And don't forget about the department stores—when they need to unload inventory, their sales can be fantastic. There are some really cute things on-line and in the catalogs—guesstimating what size your baby will need can be tricky, though. Hold off on ordering too much by mail until baby's growth slows down a bit and sizing is less erratic. That's usually around the one-year mark. You may also by shocked by the amount of clothing you receive as gifts, particularly if this is your first child. Our Girlfriend Caitlin had so much credit at babyGap from all the returns she made that she didn't actually pay for clothes at the store until her daughter started preschool.

General Wardrobe Wisdom

Before we get down to the nitty-gritty, we want to give you our basic tips about baby clothing and dressing:

Buy conservatively.

Until you've had your little babe around for a bit, there is simply no way to tell how fast she will grow, what colors she'll look good in, and what you'll like dressing her in. So don't go crazy with clothing right up front. Buy the basics. Keep tags on the clothes until you're actually going to use them. And simply accept the fact that you will be making trips to the store in the future—to make returns and to buy new stuff. Believe us, you're going to want excuses for getting out of the house, and baby stores—filled with other new moms, nursing-friendly dressing rooms, super cute stuff, and other crying infants—will be one of your favorite havens.

Think practical, not posh.

There's simply no point in paying too much attention to durability and designer names at this point. During their first few months especially, babies grow out of their clothes at light speed. They lie around all day—which does not put a lot of wear and tear on a garment. And they leak all kinds of fabric-staining body fluids. Buy the bulk of your basics from trusted, unfussy manufacturers, let baby use and abuse them, then get rid of them if they become too grungy. Besides, you may receive some of those fancy designer duds as gifts.

Don't take sizing too seriously.

Generally, sizing for baby clothes go something like this: Newborn, 3 months, 6 months, 9 months, 12 months, 18 months, 24 months. Sometimes you'll be given a size range, such as 3-6 months. Manufacturers all have their own idea of who exactly should fit in these clothes. Babies all have their own idea of how fast they're going to grow. Combine these factors, and you can see why it's darned hard to determine what will fit your baby—even after she's born.

Much as the Girlfriends would like to, we can't deliver any scientific solution here. We can say that for starters, you might want to buy a couple (and we mean a couple) of items in the "Newborn" size. Your baby will grow out of them in about five minutes. But being a new parent you'll probably want her to look somewhat presentable in the beginning—and giant baggy outfits with rolled-up sleeves can look a little sorry. (Save that for your second child.) Buy most of baby's first clothes in the 3-month size, and some in the 6-month size—he'll grow into them quickly. As for future sizing decisions—your best bet is to buy clothes that are "preshrunk," buy slightly on the big side, and HOLD ON TO THOSE RECEIPTS.

Opt for easy-on, easy-off, easy-access garments.

Specifically, we're talking about shirts and tops with wide neck openings or snaps at the neck, to help ease them over baby's head. Always go for snap or zipper closures—buttons are difficult to manipulate and can pose a choking hazard; Velcro can lose its "grip." Avoid outfits that fasten down the back—the hardware can be irritating for your baby (who will spend most of her early life on her back) and requires you to either flop baby forward or put her on her stomach to finish dressing her. Lastly, you'll want full diaper access—look for clothes that snap or zip open not just in the crotch area, but all the way down one, or ideally, both legs. A notable exception: soft, stretchy elastic-waisted pants that can be yanked down and back up in a jiffy.

Swear to buy wash-and-wear.

Unless you have a full-time laundress, avoid anything that will need to be dry-cleaned or ironed. That includes everyday coats and blouses. And your wardrobe, too, Girlfriend.

So What's a Layette, Anyway?

Long before she had any babies of her own, our Girlfriend Margot attended her very first baby shower. Margot was certainly intrigued by all the exotic gear and goodies that were unwrapped that afternoon. What mystified her most was when the mommy-to-be opened an envelope, hugged the grandmotherly type who gave it to her, and announced with a broad smile: "It's the layette."

What the heck was a layette? Was it like a bassinet? A launderette? And how much of anything could have fit in that skinny envelope, anyway? Margot wondered. For about thirty seconds.

Flash forward five years. Margot is seven months pregnant. With umpteen baby showers behind her, our Girlfriend is clued in enough to know that the layette has something to do with clothes and towels. (She now also realizes that it was a check—not some miniature wardrobe—inside that envelope all those years ago.) But Margot is still confused by the whole layette concept.

She's confused for good reason, because—though the word may sound sort of official—*layette* really doesn't have a clear definition. Some motivated salespeople will tell you the layette includes absolutely everything a new baby will need, from diapers to bottle brushes. Others will say the term refers to baby's first wardrobe. We say: Don't get all worked up about it. There is no law requiring you to buy everything on some random layette list that's handed to you. There's no law that a layette must be color-coordinated. There is no law that says layette items must all be bought at once. Lose the "layette" term altogether, if you want. Just know that you will have to buy some basic jammies, undies, rompers, and towels before or shortly after your baby arrives.

With that cleared up, here's the Girlfriends' suggested list of basics you'll need to get your newborn started:

Clothing:

4 SIDE-SNAP UNDERSHIRTS: Chances are you'll dislike these tiny T-shirts as much as we did—they have a tendency to ride up like crazy. But you'll have to use them for the first week or two until your baby's umbilical cord stump heals and falls off (yes, that does happen). Anything too tight against your baby's belly can irritate it. Since side-snap shirts slip on like a jacket, they also provide a little extra reassurance during those first couple of weeks when you're terrified to put anything over your baby's head.

8 SNAP-CROTCH UNDERSHIRTS (ALSO KNOWN AS "ONESIES," FOR ONE-PIECE UNDIES): Once that belly-button stump falls off, you'll move right on to these handy little cotton bodysuits. They will be baby's first clothing layer for a good long time; in the heat of the summer, they can be baby's only layer of clothes, day or night. *If you give birth in the summer, buy 8 short-sleeved; in winter, buy 6 short-sleeved and 2 long-sleeved. (We're not so hot on buying too many of the long-sleeved onesies—it can be a pain trying to pull another long-sleeve layer over them without the arms bunching up.)*

2 GOWNS WITH ELASTICIZED BOTTOMS: You and your baby will either love these newborn-sized sacklike pajamas—or you'll hate 'em. Fans like gowns because their open bottoms provide super-easy diaper access—a boon for middle-of-the-night changes. Antigown girls say that the garments restricted their baby's leg movement, didn't keep little legs cozy enough in winter, and—unlike most stretchies—generally had to be pulled on over baby's head. We say, buy a couple. Make sure they're made from nice, soft, stretchy material and have elasticized as opposed to drawstring bottoms (the latter could be a strangulation hazard). If you and baby like 'em, you can always buy a couple more.

6 STRETCHIES: Early on—when "bedtime" can occur just about anytime—your baby will spend most of her days and nights in these footed or footless pajama-type getups. Traditionally, stretchies were made from flame-resistant materials in order to meet sleepwear safety standards. Still widely popular, this type of stretchie tends to be generously cut, have a terry-cloth like feel, is often made from polyester, and is relatively inexpensive. For reasons the Girlfriends aren't too clear on, the government recently relaxed standards and now permits juvenile sleepwear to be made from 100 percent cotton. The "new" cotton stretchies tend to be a little bit more expensive and have a somewhat more stylish look. Keep in mind that for babies over nine months, cotton sleepwear must be snug-fitting, since a mobile child has a greater risk of brushing up against something that is flammable. *If you give birth in the late spring or early summer, you may only need 4 stretchies, since baby may spend most of her time in her undershirt.*

1–2 SLEEP SACKS: These wearable blankets essentially eliminate the need to keep a traditional blanket in the crib. This makes safety advocates happiest because loose blankets and other soft objects in the crib have been associated with an increased risk of Sudden Infant Death Syndrome (our chapter on cribs will talk more about SIDS). Several manufacturers make sleep sacks. The microfleece HALO SleepSack is a particularly attractive choice because it does not have arms and thus reduces the risk of a baby overheating, yet another factor that contributes to increased SIDS risk. (Babies generally wear light pajamas underneath.) For purchasing information, call 888-999-HALO or log on to *www.halosleep.com*. There are also some decent HALO knockoffs that are considerably less expensive. Note: Sleep sacks are generally used during the colder months; when it's warm out, pajamas alone will do.

4 PAIRS OF SOCKS: Believe it or not, you will have to choose socks carefully—most simply don't stay on babies' little feet. babyGap makes socks that have staying power without being uncomfortably tight. One more note: You won't be able to resist buying socks in all those cute colors and patterns. Eventually, though, after weeping into your baby's underwear drawer because you can't find a match for anything, you'll do what veteran Girlfriends do: Buy socks in all white. You will never have more than one old maid at any point.

4 CLOTH BIBS: You may end up using these early on to sop up all the drool and cheesy stuff that spills out of your baby's mouth. In general, avoid fancy bibs with appliqués and other darling doo-dads (use the ones you get as gifts for Thanksgiving and other show-off occasions). They're impractical and can be uncomfortable. Go for standard size, absorbent terry-cloth bibs with Velcro or snap closures. When your baby starts on solids, pick up a couple of those plastic-coated cereal bibs with the catch pocket on the bottom. They're your best shot at containing some of the gruel she'll be shooting back at you.

2 LIGHTWEIGHT CAPS: If we don't tell you this, some other well-meaning busybodies on the street will: A newborn head generally needs to keep covered. Even indoors, on occasion, since air-conditioning and scant heat can leave rooms a bit chilly at any time of year. Soft cotton knits or weaves are a good choice. Many outfits you'll get as gifts will come with matching caps of their own, so don't overbuy.

2-3 OUTDOOR HATS AND CAPS: In the winter you'll want hats that are soft, cozy, and snug to your baby's head. (On very cold days your baby should wear a hat even if the hood on her snowsuit or bunting is up, since the Girlfriends have generally found that the fit isn't close enough to the head to provide good protection.) Steer away from wool, which can be very itchy or irritating; fleece or soft polyester blends are best. A soft under-the-chin strap will help keep the hat on. In the warmer months your baby will need a sun hat as protection—the best are the caps that have flaps that go over the ears and back of the neck.

1 FLEECE SNOWSUIT: Skip those puffy, waterproof coveralls in the beginning—they're bulky, not very comfortable, and unnecessary since young babies don't go romping around in the wet, cold snow. Opt instead for a soft fleece zip-front snowsuit with legs and a hood; some actually have a zipper that converts the garment from a cozy bunting bag to a suit with legs. Lots of outdoorsy catalogs and Web sites carry fleece snowsuits—Lands' End, L.L. Bean, and Patagonia among them. The Girlfriends use these coverups year 'round. They are wonderful in winter and have kept many babies warm and happy on cool summer evenings and on over air-conditioned airplanes.

1 GOING-HOME OUTFIT: Remember that you will probably be a nervous wreck when you are ready to bring your newborn home for the first time. Pick something simple and soft that your quivering hands will be able to maneuver easily. To play it really safe, opt for an outfit that won't need to go on over your newborn's head.

Layette linens, etc.

3 RECEIVING BLANKETS: You will use these thin, square, cotton-knit, flannel, or waffle-weave blankets for everything: to swaddle your newborn, as carriage blankets, as an extra layer of warmth, as coverage when you nurse in public. Buy three soft, simple ones. We guarantee you will get more as gifts.

6 BABY WASHCLOTHS: You could use regular adult washcloths, but thinner, softer baby washcloths are less bulky and make it easier to get into baby's tiny folds, curves, and crevices.

2 HOODED TOWELS: We're including these baby-size towels with built-in hoods just because we know that a layette isn't a layette without them. Granted, babies do look cute in them—some sentimental Girlfriends couldn't bring themselves to stop using the things until their babies were old enough to do their own laundry. And we guess a hood might keep a baby a bit cozier—for the forty seconds they use it. But in general we find hooded towels (unless they are high-end and expensive) are made from very thin terry that gets soaked in an instant. Buy a couple for starters—you will no doubt get cute ones as gifts. Then move on, like we did, to nice, thick, fluffy grown-up towels.

12 CLOTH DIAPERS: Even if you will be using disposable diapers, you should buy a hefty stash of thick, prefolded cloth diapers. You will use these absorbent swatches of fabric as burp cloths, for wiping up messes, as makeshift diaper changing pads—you name it. When you no longer have babies, those old cloth diapers will become your favorite cleanup rags.

3 FITTED CHANGING-PAD COVERS: Changing-table pads come in different thicknesses and shapes. Make sure you buy covers to fit yours.

2 WATERPROOF LAP PADS: These are basically small, thin rubber sheets with a soft flannel lining on one or both sides. Before diapers became as absorbent as they are now, lap pads were the only thing that stood between a leaky baby bottom and all it came in contact with—like the baby swing cushions, the bouncy seat sling, Mom's nice trousers, etc. These days lap pads aren't the necessity they once were. But those of us who used cloth diapers or had leakage issues swear by them. Buy a couple—if you find them handy, buy more.

★　★　★

Details on the following items are included in separate chapters. We are mentioning them here because they generally fall under the layette umbrella.

2 FITTED BASSINET SHEETS

3 FITTED CRIB SHEETS

The Rest of Baby's Wardrobe

We're sure you've seen all those minuscule mannequins in baby boutique windows—done up in tiny oxford shirts and weensy jeans, Lilliputian jumpers, and bonny little blouses. This is the garb you imagine your babe will wear. This is apparel you will get as gifts.

This is not, however, what really makes sense for very young humans. All soft curves and floppy appendages, infants don't have boxy frames to hold up overalls and jumpers. They don't have slim necks around which to button cute collars. Trying to stuff their soft little legs into a pair of stiff little jeans is like trying to feed ropes of bread dough through a clarinet. The overall effect: Baby isn't as comfy as he could be. And he doesn't even look that cute—what with his pants bunched up at his chest and his neck bulging out of his shirt like some overweight bureaucrat.

Do yourself, your baby, and your photo album a favor and buy clothing that fits the reality of a young infant's body, as well as their slacker-esque lifestyle. In essence, opt for outfits that would flatter a blob of Flubber and be comfy enough for a nap on a moment's notice. Generally, we're talking about soft, stretchy cotton knits and elastic waistbands, and a distinct absence of metal clasps, scratchy lace, and other doodads that can irritate or annoy a chubby, potentially sleepy little person. It's sorta like the stuff that you would wear if you didn't have a reputation to keep up.

Some good basics include:

COTTON-KNIT, COTTON-FLEECE, OR MICROFLEECE CARDIGANS: They're easy to slip on, provide a little extra warmth, and will add a dressier touch to just about any outfit.

ONE-PIECE PLAYSUITS: These not only simplify your life, they look great on your baby. They don't ride up, they don't fall down. If you buy one-piece garments without feet, it will take longer for your baby to outgrow them. A company named Zutano makes some of the softest, most irresistible one-piece outfits on the planet. They're as soft as pj's but look a bit spiffier.

SNAP-CROTCH TOPS: If you buy some separates, opt for shirts that are actually bodysuits that snap between the legs. They stay in place and eliminate diaper and tummy exposure. If you find yourself wandering toward any kind of turtleneck (which definitely ain't the easiest thing to pull over a baby's big head), make sure you buy one that has snaps down the neck and shoulder and is made of soft stretchy cotton.

STRETCHY PANTS: Slip these over a snap-crotch shirt, and you're in business. They're cozy, comfy, easy to roll up if the legs are too long, and cute to boot. Lands' End and Hanna Andersson make nice ones. Gymboree stores also sell luxurious cotton leggings, often with coordinated tops. Colors and styles vary by season, but our Girlfriends with baby girls have especially loved their selection. (Later, when your baby shucks diapers, Gymboree makes some of the most charming, indestructable panties around.)

What's Not Necessary:

SHOES: Babies' little feet are best off unrestricted until they start walking. If you can't resist buying a pair of mini high-tops, be sure the shoes have nice, soft, flexible soles (in other words, we're talking glorified booties).

BOOTIES: We've each donated at least five single booties to the Lost and Found at our local malls. That's because the darned things don't really stay on very well. If you do give booties a whirl, slip them over a pair of thick socks; it may increase your chances of holding on to them.

DRESSES (UNLESS THEY HAVE BUILT-IN BLOOMERS): Yes, of course, baby girls *can* wear dresses. There are Girlfriends among us who wouldn't consider it a holiday or a Sunday dinner at Grandma's if their little dumpling wasn't duded up in a tiny frock and tights. We just think that dresses for everyday wear are a big pain, at least until a baby can walk on her own. You'll have to buy and futz around with tights and leggings. Most of the time the dress will end up around your little girl's neck—which isn't a great look. When your princess starts crawling, a dress will get caught under her knees, basically leaving her immobile. (Hmmm . . . that might not be such a bad thing, come to think of it.)

BULKY SWEATERS: Those pricey hand-knits sure look purty on the rack, but you'll have one devil of a time getting spit-up out of the weave without washing the whole darned thing. As a result, items like this will spend more time in the washing machine or at the dry cleaner than on your baby.

The Skinny on Laundry

If laundry has never played a big role in your life, your baby's birth will be a turning point. In the beginning, babies can go through four changes of clothing or more each day. If you have a washer and dryer in your home, many of your conscious moments will be spent thinking about putting all those soiled duds into the washer, switching them over to the dryer, folding them up, and—ha ha ha—putting it all away. If you don't have your own laundry facilities, many of your conscious thoughts will be devoted to fantasies about having such equipment. Here are some Girlfriend thoughts on the subject:

Don't wash new stuff too far in advance.

Yes, you should wash what you buy before baby wears it. Don't just dump everything into the washer as soon as you get home from buying the layette, however. There's simply no way of telling if you'll need it all or if you got the right sizes. And it isn't easy to return stuff once the tags are off and the items have been one with your washing machine. (We didn't say impossible, since our Girlfriend Eleni made this mistake and was actually able to return her stuff.) Launder a few key items before your baby is born—the bassinet sheets, a towel, a few washcloths, her going-home outfit, some undershirts, a stretchie. Then wash as you go.

To Dreft or not to Dreft.

Most parenting books, even most maternity ward nurses, will tell you that you should wash your baby's clothes with a special detergent that won't irritate your baby's delicate skin. Two of the most popular brands are Dreft and Ivory Snow. We're not going to tell you not to use this stuff. Heck, if your baby were to get a little rash, it wouldn't be the end of the world, but it sure would be upsetting for all parties, including us. What we can say is that by the time we reached our second and third kids, we not only used regular detergent, we washed their delicate ditties along with the rest of the family's soiled sweat socks and ketchup-covered T-shirts. And so far so good. If all this just sounds too reckless, you might want to consider starting out with the fancy baby detergent. Then slowly segue into something that seems almost as benign, like a fragrance-free, dye-free version of one of the big brands. If you can't bear the idea of washing baby's stuff with big old Daddy's gym towel, wash it with your delicates— you'll probably all fare just fine.

Stain removers rule!

As a responsible adult, you probably haven't had the need to "shout" out grape juice and bloodstains from your clothing. As a parent of a baby, you won't be dealing with those particular stains, either. You will, however, be in an ongoing stain battle with poop, urine, perhaps formula, and later, baby food. Enzyme-based stain removers will help. One brand that has won over the Girlfriends is Zout. Totally Toddler is another Girlfriend favorite—it smells great, works amazingly well, and comes in economical jumbo refills. It also does the trick on carpet and upholstery—a good thing to keep in mind if you've got a super-duper spitter-upper. For best results you'll have to zap stains when they are fresh and do the wash the same day. If you can't do wash at a whim, opt for an enzyme-based stain *stick*, since stain-stick-treated clothes are generally fine sitting around for up to a week.

Bleach works, too.

Bleach is fine to use on most cotton whites (check labels to make sure). Run an extra wash cycle to get the smell and any residue out. Color-safe bleaches like Clorox II are great for brightening light colors. (With the latter, try one or two garments first to check for skin sensitivity.)

Ode to the lingerie bag.

Chances are you won't be washing a lot of sexy lingerie postpartum. But these protective net bags are great for washing and keeping track of socks, booties, and other tiny baby accessories that tend to vaporize in the wash process. Just stuff the little items into the net sack, zip it closed, toss it in with the rest of the wash, and dry them all right in the bag.

A Note About Preemie Clothes

Our Girlfriend Shane was only twenty-seven weeks into her pregnancy when she went into labor and gave birth to her daughter Lucy. To say Shane and her husband, Pete, were taken by surprise is putting it lightly. They had yet to attend their childbirth class. They hadn't looked into car seats and strollers. They hadn't bought a speck of clothing. Since Shane and Pete spent the following ten weeks by Lucy's side in the hospital, there was little time to shop. Shane did most of her research and purchasing on the Internet in the wee hours of the night. Buying on-line was a particular boon, says Shane, when it came to clothing for Lucy, since preemie sizes can be difficult to track down in stores. She particularly relied on babyGap's Web site. It offered a wide selection of adorable, all-cotton newborn essentials in preemie sizes. When she needed to make returns, Shane simply dropped them off at the Gap retail store near her home. Another good source for preemie clothing, as well as other preemie gear, is the Minnesota-based Preemie Store. Call 800-676-8469 for a catalog, or log on to their Internet store (*www.preemie.com.*) BTW: Lucy did just great.

A Note About Twins

Our Girlfriend Jessie not only has twins, she herself is a twin and her sister has twins. Her advice: If you're expecting two babies, you're probably best off buying double the amount of all your layette basics. With twins, you not only have double the babies, you have half the amount of time to care for each one of them. You'll want to put convenience on top to maximize the little time you have—which means doing laundry as seldom as possible. Since twins are often on the small side compared to other newborns, you might want to buy a few more clothing items in the newborn size. Jessie warns that if you have same-sex fraternal twins, you shouldn't get caught up trying to buy different outfits and items for each child. It can be a challenge sniffing out enough stretchies you like in the right size for one child—it'll take too much time out of your life searching out different flavors for two. The exception: If you have identicals, you may actually need to color code them so you can easily tell them apart. For a wide range of tips and resource info from moms of multiples, check out the Twins and Supertwins List at *www.twinslist.org*.

CHAPTER THREE

The Cursory Nursery

Truth be told, a baby's nursery is more of an emotional shrine and glorified storage room than anything else. Tiny infants do not horse around in them. They really don't spend too much time sleeping in them, for that matter. Grown-ups might stumble in to make diaper changes or grab some supplies, but we quickly whisk baby off to where we need to be—in the kitchen, the bathroom, our bedroom. If you don't believe us, check out the home of any infant. We betcha that the nursery is the only room that's neat as a pin. That's because no one really spends much time in it.

We're telling you this because if, by chance, you don't have the room or resources to create an elaborate nursery for your new baby, no one is going to suffer. Your child will not notice if the walls aren't covered with bunny-themed wallpaper. Said child might even appreciate that fact when he or she is still in that room at the age of five. What matters most is that the space is quiet, babyproofed, and functional. If that happens to be a screened-off alcove or the former location of your currently uprooted office, so be it.

If you do choose to make a formal nursery for your baby, we think it makes the most sense to work from a somewhat neutral palette and create the "nursery" and gender-specific vibe (if you know the gender) with decorative flourishes, like an Eric Carle print, a small area rug, a cute lamp, or a pretty wallpaper border. This way it will be less expensive and easier to update the room for the next child or for the next stage in this baby's life.

Here's our list of basics:

The Crib

Because so many babies have been hurt or even killed by shoddy and poorly designed cribs in the past, the government now requires that every new crib sold in the United States meets the same exact safety standards. So regardless of what you spend on a new crib, your baby will most probably be safe (there are no guarantees, regardless of the price).

Are the Girlfriends, then, going to tell you to buy the cheapest thing out there? No. Here's our reasoning: Assuming that this is your first child and that he or she may someday have a sibling or three, you are going to want a crib that can go the distance. You will want something that is easy to use, sturdy, and dependable. That will generally cost you some extra bucks. Money well worth it, in our opinion.

Here's what you should pay more for:

- **A well-known brand name.** We're not saying you have to shell out for some high-status European label. We're talking cribs here, not handbags. We simply want you to go with a name that has an established reputation and track record in the crib industry. Kind of like opting for a Chevy or Toyota instead of some obscure, mysteriously inexpensive import from a country you can't even find on your globe. We say this because a crib is a major piece of gear with moving parts, and you'll want to know that the manufacturer will be around next year or in five years should you need parts or service. Our Girlfriend Amanda called the manufacturer when the side rail on her six-year-old crib broke, and they overnighted a new part, free of charge, no questions asked. No small deal when you're a mom with a kamikaze toddler. After visiting one or two baby furniture stores and baby superstores, the better-known brands will become familiar—a few to keep an eye out for include Child Craft, Legacy, Simmons, Sorelle, Morigeau-Lepine, Pali, and Ragazzi.

- **A side rail that can be lifted and lowered using one hand.** Remember, your baby will be monopolizing at least one of your arms most of the time. Pass up the cheaper cribs that require you to squeeze something at each end of the side rail in order to release it.

- **A knee-release side rail.** For safety reasons, cribs with one-hand-release side rails require that you also either push on a bar at the bottom of the crib with your foot or push against the crib's side rail with your knee. Nowadays, most of the better cribs use the knee-release mechanism—it's generally quieter to use and the basic design usually requires that less hardware be exposed.

- **Better performance.** We're talking specifically about how smoothly, quietly, and easily the side rail can be raised and lowered. This is no small deal, since you will be doing this action hundreds, possibly thousands of times over the next several years. The only case where this may not matter is if you and the other folks in your house are relatively tall (over 5 feet 8). Our Girlfriend Patsy tells us that neither she nor anyone else in her Amazon family ever bothers dropping the side rails to get their babes in or out of the crib. She doesn't even know how her side-rail mechanism works.

- **Durability and sturdiness.** Look for smooth finished surfaces and edges. When you shake the crib, parts shouldn't rattle too much or too loudly. This sounds unscientific, but it really can give you a feel for how well—or poorly—a crib is made. The mattress should have decent supports underneath—metal are the most durable.

Now for what you don't need.

When you go crib shopping, the salespeople will inevitably show you cribs with all kinds of other special features. Remember, this is how they make their money. Resist, Girlfriend, resist.

- **The "double drop."** This allows you to raise and lower the rails on both sides of the crib. In the midst of crib mania, you will be able to think up at least five reasons why this feature would greatly improve your life as a new mother and add to your child's overall happiness. Since we are not pregnant and are not in the store, we can't think up even one. Which is our way of saying that YOU DO NOT NEED DOUBLE-DROP SIDE RAILS. Chances are very high that if you live in an average-size home or smaller, one side of your baby's crib will be up against a wall, which would render this feature pointless. If you do live in the equivalent of the Hearst mansion and the crib is in the middle of the room, your butler won't really care if he has to walk around to one side to get the baby.

- **The under-crib drawer.** After agonizing for three weeks over whether "to drawer or not to drawer," our Girlfriend Felicia and her husband shelled out the extra bucks and special-ordered a crib just so they could have this feature. Five months later that illustrious drawer was home to a few surplus baby blankets and a moose puppet that never saw the light of day after scaring the bejeezus out of little Theo. By the time Theo was crawling, Felicia had no choice but to transform the drawer into toy storage, since emptying out its contents became Theo's favorite pastime. The moral of this story: If you have very limited dresser and storage space, this feature might be handy for a short time. But it shouldn't be a deal breaker if you find an affordable, sturdy crib you like that doesn't have this feature. P.S. Many of the higher-end cribs automatically include the drawer feature, so "to drawer or not to drawer" won't even be an issue if you are looking in this category.

- **The "convertible" option.** It seems to make so much sense—a crib that can transform into a toddler bed, and then into a twin bed! Just think of the time and money you might save. We can't think of anything sillier. First off, by the time your baby is ready for a bed, you may need that crib for your next child. Second, there is no real need for a toddler bed. If your child seems lonely or overwhelmed by a standard twin bed when the time comes to move on from the crib, buy him or her a stuffed animal. Third, who knows where you'll be and what taste you'll have when the crib is finally free and can be transformed into a twin bed. You might want to buy something altogether different.

- **A million mattress heights.** As far as we're concerned, all you need are two. The very highest spot, which you'll use when baby is essentially a lump and unable to move on his or her own. And the very bottom, where you will move the mattress the second your little sweetheart shows any ability whatsoever to roll, sit up, get up, or do anything else that might risk his catapulting himself from the crib. We take this cautious approach because adjusting the mattress height is not exactly easy. Once you or your husband curse your way through this experience, you will want to do it as infrequently as possible. This means forgetting all the middle-of-the-road slots and going straight for the bottom.

- **Fancy designs.** Ultimately, it's aesthetics that adds the most to a crib's price tag. Here we aren't going to mince words: Don't waste your brain cells or your budget seeking out the ultimate object of beauty. A crib is a crib and it will never be mistaken for a Corvette or an Eames chair. Whether you plan to have two children or twelve, this piece of furniture will ultimately end up disassembled and dust-covered in your attic or basement. And because cribs aren't safe bets as heirlooms, chances aren't good that you'll pass this relic on to your grandchildren. Even if you are a product of the dot.com boom before it went bust, buy something that is simple and appealing, slap some pretty bedding on it, and put all of that extra cash toward a piece of furniture for the house that has some real staying power.

Where to Buy Your Crib

You can score a crib from any number of places—department stores, grown-up furniture stores, baby furniture stores, baby superstores, on the Internet. Let us explain why it makes the most sense to buy your crib at a baby furniture store. From what the Girlfriends have observed, these places tend to have "exclusives" on the better name brands. And in general, these brands have higher quality mechanisms and overall construction than cribs sold at discount and superstores. This is true whether you buy their simplest model or their most elaborate. If you pay a visit to both types of stores, you'll see that if you opt for a basic model from a high-end maker at the specialty stores, you can pay roughly the same as you will if you buy a middle-of-the-road product from a mediocre maker at the superstore. (You may even pay less at a specialty store if you buy a crib on clearance.) We think the choice is obvious: Buy the lower-end crib from the higher-end manufacturer. You'll get better construction and better performance, albeit without some of the window dressing. Based on the Girlfriends' experience, specialty stores also stand a better chance of standing behind their product if you have a problem.

Many of the better stores will deliver and assemble the crib for a very modest fee. That's a big deal because cribs can be a huge pain in the neck to put together. YOU AND YOUR HUSBAND SHOULD WATCH CAREFULLY HOW THE CRIB GUYS PUT THE THING TOGETHER SO YOU'LL KNOW HOW TO DO IT WHEN YOU TAKE THE CRIB OUT OF STORAGE FOR YOUR NEXT BABY. If you or someone in your life happens to be handy and you don't need any special tutoring, go for the best deal you can find once you know what model and make you want. If that deal ends up being offered by catalog or over the Internet, be sure that you have seen and tried a similar model crib made by the same manufacturer in person first, either at a local retailer or at a Girlfriend's house.

In recent years home-design catalogs and trendy design stores have started selling some very pretty cribs of their own. These cribs might actually be made by big crib manufacturers and then be sold under a "private label" name. They might be made by one of the merchandiser's own vendors. Either way, we're not crazy about the idea. There's no telling how long a merchandiser will remain enchanted with the crib business and if parts and service will be available in the future. If the crib is indeed made for a retailer by a major manufacturer, you are simply adding a middle-man to the picture and leaving room for some serious buck passing (and price hiking). We also think it makes good sense from a safety and functionality perspective to go with a manufacturer that considers cribs its specialty, not merely a dalliance.

When to Buy the Crib

In most cases, you will have to order your crib in advance. Basic domestic brands may only take a couple days or weeks to arrive. Fancy imports may take twelve weeks or more to make an appearance. Just to play it safe, the crib should be one of the first items you start shopping around for, and you should try to place the order sometime around your sixth or seventh month. If you just can't pull this off for some reason, don't sweat it. As you'll soon read, you probably won't be using the crib until quite a while after your little celebrity makes her debut.

Secondhand Woes

We really really really REALLY want to come straight out and demand that you buy your baby a brand-new crib. This way you can be sure that the one you are using meets current federal safety standards (which have changed significantly for cribs over the years), has all its parts and pieces, and is in mint condition.

We're dealing with the real world here, however. And a quick survey among the Girlfriend ranks tells us that regardless of what the ideal is, many expectant moms are going to go ahead and borrow or accept a hand-me-down crib anyway. If there's a big red arrow flashing over your head this very minute, at least take these precautions:

Borrow from someone you know. Under no circumstances should you purchase a used crib from a garage sale, secondhand store, or Web site, since you won't be able to determine much, if anything, about it.

Borrow the newest crib possible. Borrow only from someone who purchased a crib new within the last three or four years herself. Older cribs stand a much greater chance of not meeting the most recent government safety standards. They could be covered with lead paint. The slats may be spaced widely enough to trap a baby's head between them. High, spindled corner posts pose a serious strangulation hazard. Wear and tear also takes a toll and can eventually compromise how sturdy a crib is and how well it will function.

Check for recalls and alerts. The www.dannyfoundation.org Web site, which promotes crib safety, posts an ongoing list, as well as comprehensive crib safety information. If you register with the site, they will e-mail automatically when a crib recall or warning is issued.

Get instructions and use the right hardware. A crib that is assembled incorrectly or with makeshift parts can be deadly. If your friend no longer has the literature that came with the crib or if some parts, screws, etc., are missing, call the manufacturer. Order a new set of instructions. If replacement parts are not available, don't make substitutions. Take a pass.

The Crib Mattress

From start to finish, buying a crib mattress typifies the lunacy that can overtake the baby-gear buying experience. You begin by cheerfully asking to be shown what you need to buy for your crib. Not so fast, Girlfriend. What just five minutes ago may have seemed like a straightforward decision suddenly morphs into a Ph.D.-worthy ordeal. Quickly ushering you past a few humbly priced foam mattresses (the low-rent neighborhood of the mattress universe), your salesperson takes you to her showcase of high-tech innerspring mattresses, officiously throwing around terms like "coil count" and "Staph-Guard." You begin to smirk a little, wondering just how much back support and staph-fighting protection a newly minted baby really needs. But then come the clincher phrases: "Sudden Infant Death Syndrome," "suffocation" "safety," "risk." Without batting an eye you become the proud new owner of an "ultra-prima-dura-super-elastic-safe-and-secure" mattress for the "bargain" price of $210.

Spare yourself the angina and the expense. Don't depend on a salesperson for advice (unless you are blood related). Listen instead to the American Academy of Pediatrics, the Sudden Infant Death Syndrome Alliance, the Consumer Product Safety Commission, and your Girlfriends about what you really need to know and care about when buying a new crib mattress:

- **It must be very firm.** According to the SIDS Alliance, the best way to test the firmness of a coil or foam mattress is to stand the mattress on end and hold it between the palms of your two hands. (Your hands will be touching the wide sleeping surfaces, the skinny sides will be facing toward and away from you.) With your hands directly opposite each other at the center of the mattress, press. Comparing mattresses should give you some firmness context.

- **It must fit your crib.** To prevent your baby from becoming trapped in any way, make sure the crib mattress fits quite snugly in the crib.

- **It must have a nonporous (for example, vinyl) and non-padded covering.** To minimize the potential for cracks and tears down the road, choose a mattress with a cover that is absent of frays and double or even triple laminated. Yes, it sounds like we are recommending that your baby sleep on the equivalent of a bus-station bench. And essentially, we are. Cushiness equals danger when it comes to crib mattresses. Do not be seduced by how "comfy" or cozy a mattress looks.

- **The upshot: A high-density, good-quality foam mattress will do the job.** And since they tend to weigh less than the innerspring mattresses, foam mattresses reduce the torture quotient when it's time to change baby's sheets. Don't buy the cheapest thing out there—go for a well-known brand like Colgate and pay on the higher end of the foam spectrum. (Contrary to what some people—mostly salespeople—claim, foam mattresses can be passed down to younger siblings. The SIDS Alliance simply recommends that you make sure the mattress is still firm before you use it again.) If you can't find a good foam mattress or don't want to go that route, conduct the same firmness test on innerspring mattresses and go for something in the middle price range with a well-known name like Serta, Sealy, or Simmons. If you're borrowing or inheriting a crib—and you know our caveats about that—be a sport and buy your baby his own mattress.

Crib Accoutrements

Once you've bought a lovely crib, it's only natural you'll want to make it as cozy and cushy as can be for your little angel. Utter these words to someone who knows something about crib safety, and his or her head may just spin off his or her shoulders.

We'll spare you that sight and simply tell you why the cozy, cushy, comfy approach to crib decor is about as P.C as giving cigarettes to a five-year-old. Decades of research has revealed that soft, pillowy surfaces and poor ventilation not only increase the risk of suffocation, they can cause babies to rebreathe carbon-dioxide-laden air that has pooled around their face. This, research has shown, can heighten the risk of Sudden Infant Death Syndrome (SIDS)—the inexplicable death of sleeping infants that usually occurs within the first year of life.

Since experts don't want soft surfaces and objects in the crib area, these findings have simplified your job in the decorating department. Simply put: The less you buy, the better. True to the

American way, however, an entirely new "anti-SIDs" industry has found ways to sop up that surplus energy and cash. Page through any baby-gear catalog and you may find a number of far-out products touted to "prevent SIDS."

First of all, **there is no known way of preventing SIDS. There are simply ways of reducing risk. Primary among these: putting babies to sleep on their backs, eliminating their exposure to secondhand smoke, avoiding soft or loose bedding in the crib, and not overheating them or the room where they sleep.** The startling truth is that, according to prominent SIDS experts, some of the anti-SIDS paraphernalia that's being peddled may actually increase a child's risk of harm. SO DON'T BOTHER WITH THIS STUFF. REALLY.

With all that cleared up, here's

What You Need:

3 FITTED SHEETS: You can buy these to match the rest of your crib bedding or simply pick out a few separately packaged sheets in a coordinating color. Opt for sheets that have elastic all the way around, as opposed to just on the corners. They will stay on the mattress more securely. We think Jersey knit or thin flannel are a nicer option than the flat weave sheets—they have a softer touch and they're stretchier, which makes them easier to get onto the crib mattress.

What You Might Want:

CRIB SKIRT: Cribs have a lot of hardware down below, and a skirt does an excellent job of covering all that up. The skirt also hides all the stuff you might decide to store under the crib—a key point if you're tight on space, especially if you didn't go for that crib drawer option. Go to town choosing whatever pattern you like.

A WEARABLE SLEEP SACK: Since the goal is to keep as little in a crib as possible for the first year of a child's life, safety experts recommend skipping the crib blanket and simply dressing your baby warmly instead. Lightweight pajamas are usually adequate for the spring and fall (or summer if you have air-conditioning). In the winter you may want to use something called a sleep sack, which is like a mini fleece sleeping bag your baby essentially wears to bed. We talk more about that in the layette section. If you do insist on using a crib blanket, go for something very lightweight and that is free of any strings or extra loose weaving that can get caught on something. Tuck it in at the end where your baby's feet are and on both sides. Let the blanket come up no higher than your baby's armpits.

MOBILE: This may be one of the few toys a newborn baby actually appreciates. Even if the enchantment lasts for just two minutes at a shot, that still grants you enough time to run to the bathroom and pee. So we say it's money well spent. To achieve the desired effect, however, be careful about the mobile you pick out. It's all well and good if it looks pretty to you, but what's important is that the thing is interesting to your baby. Which means *the engaging parts of the mobile should be facing down toward your baby, not just out toward you.* Sounds obvious, but you'd be amazed by how many mobile designers—especially young *artistes* who churn out the high-end objects d'art—miss that important point. Crucial Safety Thing: As soon as your baby can sit up in her crib, you must remove the mobile. All is not lost, however. If she still finds it amusing, attach it above the changing table, and the diaper changer of the moment will benefit from the distraction.

What You Should Skip/What's Unnecessary:

BUMPERS: These pads, which line the inside rail of the crib, are supposedly intended to prevent baby from clunking her precious head or getting a limb caught between the slats. Frankly, most of us buy bumpers because they make the crib look snazzy. Now, wouldn't ya know it, safety experts are suggesting that bumpers may actually be more of a hazard than a help, due to the whole soft bedding-SIDS connection. If you absolutely cannot be persuaded to forgo this frill (which the Girlfriends really urge you to do), go for flat, thin bumpers as opposed to big, cushy, puffy ones. Make sure the bumper you choose fits your crib, and that it ties to the crib from both its top and bottom edges. Crib bumpers must be removed as soon as your baby starts to pull up. They become quasi-step stools for little Houdinis intent on escaping.

SLEEP POSITIONERS OF ANY SORT: Babies under one year of age should only be put to sleep on their backs, and they need nothing to help them achieve this miraculous feat. So ignore whatever you may see on store shelves; SIDS experts believe they are not only ineffective but may actually be dangerous. If you should come across something that's designed to keep a baby sleeping on its side (side sleepers are a very popular hand-me-down), avoid it: It's a throwback from the day (like about five minutes ago) when side sleeping was considered the way to go. It no longer is. Period.

WATERPROOF SHEETS: These are basically large, thin, flat pieces of rubbery, waterproof material with a fabric or flannel coating on one or both sides. Sometimes they are called "crib pads." The idea is that you're supposed to lay them down on top of the crib mattress before you put on the sheet. They're an option for clean freaks, but not really necessary. Most crib mattresses these days—and the ones you should be buying, anyway—have nonporous exteriors, so it's no big deal if they're exposed to a bit of baby leakage.

MATTRESS PADDING: Back to the whole soft-bedding issue, don't use anything to soften or puff up the mattress surface—not sheepskin, a baby feather bed, not thick mattress covers. If you just can't stop yourself from buying one of those waterproof mattress covers with the quilty stuff on one side, buy the thinnest, least puffy one available.

CRIB BEDDING SETS: Many of us were lured into buying expensive bedding sets. Almost all of us ended up regretting it, for the simple reason that the main item you're really shelling out for in these ensembles is an elaborate and beautiful crib quilt. And, of course, we all quickly realized that these crib quilts couldn't go anywhere near our young babies when they were in their cribs. You know, it's that SIDS-soft bedding thing. Most of our quilts ended up hanging over the back of a rocker or sitting in the nursery closet. Spare yourself the expense and buy your bedding à la carte.

PILLOWS, STUFFED ANIMALS, ETC.: Remember, nothing soft in the crib but your baby.

Baby's First Real Sleeping Spot

It's perfectly safe and appropriate to put a healthy newborn baby in a separate room in her own crib right from day one. The reality is you probably won't do it. At least not with your first child.

For starters, you will be too paranoid to let your tiny newborn out of your sight for more than a minute. (It's the same instinct that will make you nuts about putting your infant in a rear-facing car seat.) Your newborn will also spend a good part of his first nights on earth crying, squirming, feeding, or otherwise rousing the household. And you will quite simply be too exhausted to be traipsing back and forth from your room to his in order to suffer and drool along with him. Besides just giving up and sleeping on the floor of the baby's nursery (as our Girlfriend Casey did with her second child), the obvious solution is to keep your newborn in your room. Your best and safest choices include:

Best Bets

A BASSINET: A smallish basket that usually sits on a stand, a bassinet has a tiny mattress of its own and is often done up with a fluffy skirt and pastel bows. Most any infant, no matter how cone-shaped his head is from delivery or how much he resembles Herbert Hoover, looks simply angelic and saintly lying in one of these things. If someone you know has a relatively new and sturdy bassinet that she is willing to lend, grab it. It will serve you well. Stay away from heirlooms, however. Though they look enchanting, old bassinets can be very rickety and may even be covered in lead paint. Our Girlfriend Linda put her newborn Nate in a bassinet "everyone in the family had used for generations." She awakened in the middle of the night to a crash, only to find that Nate had fallen through the bottom of the bassinet and landed on the floor. If you buy a new bassinet, steer away from the bargain-basement brands. They can be unstable. Graco makes a decent bassinet that comes with sheets and a nice-sized storage basket underneath. With its wheels in one position, you can roll baby from room to room. With the wheels up, the bassinet can be rocked with a cradle-like motion. Safety thing: Whatever brand you buy, the sides of any bassinet should be vented so air will be able to circulate freely around your baby.

A PORTABLE PLAY YARD: Some portable play yards (we are heavily inclined toward the Graco Pack 'N Play, since it's had a better safety record than many) come with a bassinet feature—an insert that suspends from the top rails of the play yard and allows your baby to sleep high up and easily within your reach. If you are not obsessed with aesthetics and have space to spare in your bedroom, it's a great alternative to shelling out for a separate piece of equipment. Some play yards come with one fitted sheet. If yours does, buy an extra crib sheet specifically made for portable play yards if you intend to use it as your bassinet. If your play yard doesn't come with a fitted sheet, buy two fitted play yard sheets.

THE CO-SLEEPER: The most well-known co-sleeper, the Arm's Reach, looks kind of like a portable play yard, but it is designed so one side opens onto your own bed. Baby has his own safe sleep area but is, as the name implies, just an arm's reach away when you want to feed him. (Straps keep the co-sleeper flush to your mattress so the baby won't fall into the crack.) If you like the idea of sleeping with your baby, it's a safer alternative to keeping him or her in your own bed. If you are physically disabled or are recovering from a very difficult birth, a co-sleeper may just be manna from heaven. If you only intend to keep your baby in your room for a short time, however, it may not be worth the investment. Co-sleepers are somewhat pricey, they are big and bulky, and contrary to what the packaging implies, they really don't double as portable play yards since they are anything but easy to put up and take down. Our Girlfriend Melissa's husband, Bill, actually had to attack their co-sleeper with a hammer in order to dismantle it. She didn't know he had it in him.

Don't Bother

A CRADLE: They sure look quaint, but we're not big fans. Cradles can be expensive, they are generally heavy, and in some cases—especially older vintage pieces, of which there are many—they can be unsturdy. Additionally, some older models have solid—as opposed to slatted—sides, which may reduce air circulation and pose a potential hazard for Sudden Infant Death Syndrome.

MOSES BASKET: You'll find these storybook-adorable baby baskets at froufrou boutiques—right next to the handmade mobiles that babies hate and the chintz diapers bags that can't be cleaned. Forget them. They are not only impractical (you should never even attempt to lift a Moses basket by its pretty little handles while your baby is inside), some sport enough soft bedding to make any good SIDS researcher swallow his own tongue. To make matters worse, the handles of some Moses baskets can actually droop over into where baby is, posing a possible strangulation hazard.

Furniture and Accessories

Dresser

Baby furniture ain't cheap. It generally won't win any awards for aesthetics, either. But the stuff does have its advantages: It's generally sturdy, child-safe, and designed with functionality in mind. If you've got money to burn, by all means buy a few pieces. If you're inclined to go the Girlfriend route, however, buy a standard chest of drawers. It will probably cost you less and you'll ultimately get more use out of it. Keep the following mommy- and baby-friendly features in mind:

STURDY STATURE. The piece should ideally be wider than it is tall, in order to avoid a tipping hazard. In any case, be sure to secure the back of the chest to the wall (see the chapter on childproofing for info on furniture anchors).

A NONTOXIC, CHIP-FREE FINISH. A laminated top will make the piece particularly easy to maintain. Ask a salesperson or the manufacturer for details.

BABY-FRIENDLY CURVES AND CORNERS. Don't obsess about finding something with completely rounded corners. Not even all baby furniture has this feature these days. Simply try to find a piece that has gentle angles, finished edges and hardware, and is free of any details that could catch a child's clothing or pinch little fingers.

FIXED DRAWER PULLS. It's ideal if you can find a dresser that has no drawer pulls at all. Otherwise, make sure that the drawer pulls can't be unscrewed or pulled off easily, since they can present a possible hazard for your baby.

DRAWER STOPS: These prevent drawers from pulling all the way out of the chest.

Changing Table

Falls from changing tables are one of the most common causes of injury in young babies. Just removing your hand or turning your back for a second can open the door for big trouble. But the Girlfriends would be big fat liars if we told you we have all played it safe by changing our babies on the floor or on the bed. That would have been cruel and unusual punishment, especially for those of us recovering from C-sections or blessed with naturally bad backs. Besides, we think it's nice to have a clean, well-equipped spot where you can comfortably tackle diaper duty and other tasks that can be sort of tricky in the beginning, such as nail clipping, umbilical-stump swabbing, and onesie-changing. So we give changing tables the "thumbs up." AS LONG AS YOU KEEP AT LEAST ONE HAND ON THE BABY AT ALL TIMES AND MAINTAIN A LOW LEVEL OF PARANOIA WHENEVER YOUR CHILD IS ON THE CHANGING TABLE. When your baby gets bigger and stronger, and begins to bully you at diaper-changing time, you will ultimately end up forsaking the changing table for the floor or a big bed anyway.

Now let's talk about changing-table choices. The trend these days is the combo changing table/dresser. The idea is that it saves you the space and trouble of buying two separate pieces. We're not sold. These pieces don't generally have enough space to hold all of baby's clothes and all your diaper paraphernalia. In many cases parents end up buying a separate chest of drawers anyway. Combo pieces are expensive (we're talking about $600 and up for better quality stuff). And even when you remove the changing table hardware, they still look like, well, changing tables.

The other popular choice these days is to simply forgo any kind of formal changing table. Lots of mommies fare pretty well by fastening a contoured changing pad (snugged within a terry cover) to the top of a waist-high dresser; stashing the diapers on the floor, in a top drawer, or in a nearby cabinet; and calling it a day.

Unfashionable as it is, the Girlfriends like the traditional, stand-alone, open-shelved changing tables—the ones with a single drawer up top are particularly nice. Plenty of these sell for under $200. They give you one central spot to keep baby's diapers, toiletries, etc. They also have something that many of the combo pieces don't have: a rail around the changing surface, which makes it just a little harder for an accident to happen (EVEN THOUGH YOU WILL NEVER TAKE YOUR HANDS OFF YOUR BABY IN THE FIRST PLACE WHILE HE IS UP THERE.) When your baby gets old enough and curious enough to start flinging changing-table contents around the room, stash the diapers and linens in baskets to make them harder to get at. Hands-off items like diaper balm, lotions, etc., can be kept in the changing table drawer or up out of reach in a clip-on diaper caddy. This piece does have a limited lifetime. But it's relatively inexpensive and small enough that you won't mind storing the thing upstairs in the attic until the next baby comes. If you can't bring yourself to do even that, follow Girlfriend Shelly's lead: Move the changing table down near the back door and use it as a shoe and boot rack.

Glider

Just days after discovering she was pregnant, our Girlfriend Amanda came upon a rather intriguing oak rocking chair at a small New England antique shop. It sat low to the ground, had a cane seat, and no arms. A brief interrogation of the proprietor revealed that this unusual item was, in fact, a nursing rocker from the 1820s. Convinced it was karma, Margot shelled out $50, proudly brought home her first official piece of "baby" booty, and placed it in what would soon be the nursery. Over the coming months Amanda would fantasize about sitting in this little rocker, lovingly nursing her newborn child.

When Amanda hobbled home from the hospital with her newborn son and one doozy of an episiotomy, the first thing her eyes fixed upon was that charming 1820s nursing rocker. Considering how high the hair stood up on her neck, she might as well have been looking at an electric chair. This newly enlightened mother couldn't imagine bending her knees enough to reach the seat of that rocker, much less putting her wounded bottom on that hard cane surface.

Within five minutes Amanda's husband was on the phone with the baby store ordering one of those big, clumsy, expensive glider chairs Amanda had actually sneered at while shopping for her other baby gear. Because these new parents had to take whatever was in stock, the glider had the ugliest bunny-patterned pillows known to man. Amanda never loved a piece of furniture more in her life. Countless Girlfriend moms feel the same way, whether they nurse or bottlefeed their babies.

This little fable is our long, drawn-out way of telling you that YOU SHOULD BUY YOURSELF A VERY COMFORTABLE PLACE TO SIT WITH AND FEED YOUR BABY. BECAUSE THIS WILL ESSENTIALLY BECOME YOUR THRONE FOR THE FORSEEABLE FUTURE. The best option is a glider, which is similar to a rocker but gently slides back and forth instead of rocking. You can purchase a glider at just about any baby store. No need to go top of the line, but do invest in a chair that has arms, so your own arms have support while you are holding your babe. And pay the extra money to get cushions for the seat and back, as well as on the arms of the chair, so you don't bonk baby's head (which will easily happen, especially as he gets longer). Skip the big, pricey ottoman that comes with the glider.

It takes up a lot of room and the same job can be done by a nice little nursing stool (see below).

Nursing Stool

This is an inclined wooden footrest that helps take some of the strain off your back while you are nursing or just sitting. We guess you could put your tootsies up on a short stack of books, but the stool looks a little nicer and will be there when you need it. Medela makes a nice, well-priced one.

Bookshelf

Even a small bookcase can be squeezed into tiny bedrooms. You'll enjoy having a place to stash the beginnings of baby's first library and a surface on which to perch all those mementos and framed photos. Consider picking up something at one of those unfinished furniture places and having your hubby paint it some cheerful hue. (You'll have a legit permission slip to get out of all painting and staining, since pregnant women really shouldn't be exposed to the fumes.) Make sure that you anchor the back of the bookcase to the wall to prevent a tipping hazard.

Toy Storage

You won't have major storage needs at first, but you may be shocked by how many rattles, chew toys, and stuffed animals come pouring into the house. And without a designated storage spot for this stuff, you can count on clutter. Skip the toy trunk; things just get lost in there. Go for cubbies, plastic laundry baskets—anything that will make it easy for you and eventually your child, to get things up off the floor.

A Diaper Pail

You will definitely need a designated receptacle for your baby's soiled diapers. See our strong opinions on the subject in our "Changing Scene" chapter.

A Trash Basket

Opt for something small, plastic and either round or oval—the fewer sharp corners in a baby's room, the better. You can use this for general junk as well as pee-pee diapers, since they don't tend to smell.

Something for Dirty Laundry

You can go ahead and buy an actual hamper; make sure the lid isn't so heavy it will hurt little fingers if it comes down on them. Frankly—and this may offend some of you sensitive types—most of us just stuck a laundry basket in the nursery. The thing moved back and forth to the laundry room so often, it made more sense. (If you're concerned about aesthetics and have a closet in the nursery, stick the laundry basket on the floor in there.)

A Lamp

Here's an obvious one: Flipping on a big, bright overhead light in the middle of the night to change a diaper or soothe a crier is not a good idea. If it doesn't startle the heck out of your baby, it might convince him that sleep time is over and it's time to party. A small lamp also sets a nice, calm vibe for bedtime stories, feeding, and quiet time. If you've decided to stick with a somewhat neutral palette for your baby's room, this is one nursery embellishment that packs a nice punch. It's not the worst idea to buy something sort of cute and babyish. Make sure it's sturdy, hard to tip over, has a flame-retardant shade, and uses a low-watt bulb (about 40 watts is good). If you can't find a way to keep the cord and outlet out of a toddler's reach (like slipping it behind a night table or dresser), you might consider using a wall sconce or putting a dimmer switch on your overhead light instead. Our Girlfriend Caitlin's husband installed dimmer switches throughout their apartment, which made pacing up and down the halls during those sleepless nights a tad less jarring for all concerned.

Music

One of the nicest baby gifts our Girlfriend Shelly received was a little Fisher-Price tape player with a handful of Raffi and Pete Seeger tapes. She kept that colorful little tape player on her daughter Jody's changing table, toted it onto the floor during playtime, and brought it along when it was time for a bath. Little Jody just loved it. There was something about the immediacy and closeness of the music that totally delighted her. When Jody was older, she used it all by herself. Of course, you can also put a small boom box in the nursery. Anything is preferable to the tinny tunes that drone from many pieces of "deluxe" baby gear.

Monitor

Because this is your first baby, you will want to hear every peep and gurgle your angel makes. (My, how things change the second, third, and fourth time around.) A baby monitor—which has a transistor that stays near the baby and a receiver that stays with you—will help you accomplish this feat and then some. You might pick up your neighbor's cordless phone conversations, or the mix of boom box blare and baby cries coming from the building across the street. City-dwelling Girlfriends seem to complain the most about this interference. Our Girlfriend Felicia bought and returned three different baby monitors, with multiple channels, in her attempt to avoid accidentally eavesdropping on her neighbors, to no avail. This means other people were probably hearing her, as well.

Is a baby monitor worth all this headache, then? (Assuming you are not a voyeur.) Yes and no. If your bedroom is on the same floor as where your baby is sleeping, there's certainly no reason to have the thing on all night. You might end up running to the baby and waking him when all he was doing was passing a little gas. If you live in a smallish apartment where it will be virtually impossible *not* to hear your baby's crying, you can skip this expense. If you live in a house, the occasions when you will want a monitor are when the baby is napping during the day and you want to sit outside on the patio or do some laundry down in the basement. Do not go crazy with this purchase, however. There is no need for one of those video baby monitors. And, unless your baby has a preexisting medical condition, the same goes for those gizmos that monitor your baby's breathing. Rather than making you worry less, these over-the-top apparatuses will make you obsess that much more.

FEATURES TO LOOK FOR: When you buy your monitor, handy features to look for include a display that lights up on the receiver when the baby cries or makes noise. This way you can have friends over for dinner and keep tabs on the baby, without subjecting your guests to the sounds of your baby's evening sonata. Get a monitor that has a couple of channels, too, so you at least have a chance of escaping interference. Rechargeable receivers will help you cut down on battery consumption.

CAN YOU RECOMMEND A BRAND? In terms of interference, the Girlfriends have had good and bad experiences with many different brands. Your best strategy is to buy something with the basic features you need and see how it works. The Fisher-Price Sounds 'n Lights monitor is a good place to start.

Ventilation

If you don't have central air-conditioning, think about how you're going to control the temperature in the nursery when the weather gets warm. An individual window air conditioner can make a small room like a nursery too frigid. Without anything, however, a nursery can become stiflingly hot—which is very dangerous, particularly for babies under one year of age. Our solution? Have a ceiling fan installed. On everything but the steamiest nights (when you might move the baby into another air-conditioned room), it will do the job safely and gently. If you choose to go this route, get the disruptive task of installing it done before baby moves into the nursery. Whatever you do, don't wait until you're all baking like potatoes and your electrician is vacationing on Lake Powell.

Window Covering

Decorative drapes might be optional, but a light-obscuring shade isn't. The longer your baby thinks it's nighttime, the happier you'll all be (at least when said baby finally discovers nighttime is for sleeping). Notice we said "shade"—it's the simplest option that's safe for a baby. Venetian blinds and other window-wear may have strings, cords, or slats that can present a serious strangulation hazard.

Top Ten Answers to "How Can I Help?"

10. Tell Mom how thin she looks already.

9. Volunteer to drop off and pick up Dad's dry cleaning once a week.

8. Show up prepared to clean the kitchen or hold the baby or hold the mommy, whichever looks most needy at the time.

7. Drop off a casserole or soup, or just run by Boston Market or Pollo Loco and drop off the goodies without seeming to notice that Mommy hasn't shaved her legs or washed her hair in far too long.

6. Volunteer to go with Mom and baby to their first pediatrician's visit. There is a shot involved (hepatitis) so it will be traumatic. If Dad's not available, you will need to drive and comfort all parties.

5. Drop off a Starbucks or some other delicious eye-opening drink around 9:00 A.M. to help get Mommy through the second half of her day (which began around 3:00 A.M).

4. E-mail the latest gossip and lots of sweet inquiries about the new baby to Mom. She will probably be hiding from the phone like a vampire hides from belladonna, but she will be wide awake and in search of companionship at about 5:00 A.M.

3. Bribe someone to make a house call for a manicure/pedi-
    cure for the new mom. Encourage very short nails and top-
    coat only. Splurge on the toenails, since she'll be seeing them
    for the first time in ages.

2. Assure Mom that she is dropping weight so fast that she
    shouldn't even think of pulling out her Tae Bo tapes for
    another season or so. Remind nursing moms that about
    twenty of those extra postpartum pounds are in her breasts.

1. Promise her that you'd tell her if she was acting postpartum-
    ish and then seal your lips. Of course she's acting crazy,
    wouldn't you?

CHAPTER FOUR

The Changing Scene

In the beginning a changing table is really a new parent's "operating table"—a clean, organized spot where all kinds of delicate activities can be handled with utmost care and concentration. It is where you'll swab your newborn's umbilical cord stump, clean goopy stuff from his tiny eyes, and tend to his healing circumcision, if need be. It is where you will anoint him after the bath, comb what peach fuzz he has on his head, and pull tiny clothes onto his body. It is also, of course, where you will change about a zillion diapers.

Since all of this must be done without ever turning your back, walking away, having less than one hand on your baby, or even blinking too slowly, the trick is having every supply you could possibly need, right at your fingertips. Here's our A-list of supplies and equipment, plus some tactical tips.

The Changing Table

As we said earlier, if space allows, we think the best option is a plain, old-fashioned changing table with a barrier rail and open shelving (a storage drawer up top is a nice plus but not a necessity). Yes, this piece of furniture offers somewhat limited use, but it will provide lots of room for supplies, linens, and towels, and will be relatively inexpensive compared to a fancy combination changing table / dresser. When your baby gets mobile and more curious, stashing supplies in baskets on the changing table shelves will make them less accessible. Should you instead choose to install a changing pad on top of a dresser, keep in mind that you will need to have an easy-to-access spot for diapering and hygiene essentials. If you do not want to sacrifice the top drawer of the bureau for this purpose, you might want to put up a small supply shelf just to the side of the dresser (don't do it directly above, since it could bonk your baby's head when he becomes more mobile; falling objects could also bonk *him*). You could also simply place the dresser directly adjacent to another similarly high piece of furniture (like a bookshelf) and use that surface for supplies.

Contoured Changing Pad

With their raised edges and considerable heft, contoured changing pads are a big improvement over the thin, flat, lightweight changing pads that come with many changing tables. Buying one of these is especially worthwhile if you wind up with a changing table that doesn't have a guardrail (the raised edges won't replace your vigilance, they will merely enhance it) or if you intend to transform the top of a dresser into your changing surface. The classic contoured changing pad is made by a company called Rumble Tuff, but there are a variety of similar items on the market these days. Make sure the one you choose has a nonskid bottom (this usually involves a layer of foam on the underside) and is designed so the pad itself—not the cover—is what attaches to the top of your changing surface (though this is not a mandatory measure if your changing table has a guardrail). Also make sure it fits your changing surface—these babies are bulky. Lastly, the changing pad should have a strap that secures your baby in place. (It's a safety must, but to tell the real-dark truth, we haven't met a mom yet who has actually used the safety strap on her baby after the first week or two. We use our hands, our eyes, and our good sense to hold our little ones in place and to make sure they don't fall.)

Satellite Changing Stations

Unless you live in a small house or apartment, we think it's a great idea to have more than one changing spot in the house. Having such a satellite changing station will make it unnecessary to schlep to baby's room every time you need to change her diaper. This, in turn, will make you a nicer, happier mommy, and may actually make your husband more inclined to take on the task. You will, as a result, have a happier marriage, become perfect parents, and will feel so good about yourselves and your life, you might just choose to volunteer to build housing for the homeless. The world will be a better place. Okay, maybe we're getting a little carried away. But it is a worthwhile concept. There's really no need to have an additional changing table. An extra contoured changing pad will do the job very well. Alternatively, we also love the portable play yards that have a changing table or even simply a bassinet

insert. Depending upon the size of your home, you should ideally have at least one changing set up on each floor (this
includes your main changing table).

Changing Pad Covers

Changing pad covers are fitted terry-cloth sheets that go over
your changing pad. They make the pad cozier and more comfortable for your baby. They also absorb some of the runoff from
leaky diapers, unforeseen waterworks, and surprise spit-ups. If
you have one pad, buy about three covers, since you'll be making
frequent changes, especially in the beginning. If you have multiple changing pads, two covers for each (including the main
changing table pad) should be ample supply. Make sure you
choose covers that will fit your pad; contoured pads usually
require covers specifically designed to accommodate their shape
and size.

Supply Caddy

These small plastic caddies generally clip on to the side of your
changing table. They aren't a necessity, but they help keep small
items and diapering essentials close at hand (we give specifics
below), and enhance the storage capacity of your changing table.
A supply caddy is also great for your "satellite" changing stations
elsewhere in the house. A few of the Girlfriends have used those
shower caddies with the tall handle for holding diaper supplies
and toting them around the house.

The Right Supplies

CLOTH DIAPERS: As we mentioned in the layette chapter, you should keep about a dozen soft, prefolded cloth diapers on hand for cleanup and other "raglike" purposes. Your changing table is the ideal place to store them. One great way to put them to work: Lay a clean cloth diaper on your covered changing pad in the spot where baby's bottom will be during changes. If your babe turns out to be a big spitter upper, you may even want to keep a cloth diaper under her head during changes, as well. Should there be a leak of some sort, chances are good that you'll be able to simply replace the cloth diaper instead of changing the entire changing pad cover. Another handy tactic for mother's of baby boys: Something about the changing table inspires wee lads to turn on the waterworks. Laying a cloth diaper over your son's privates during changes will prevent you—and the rest of the changing area—from getting sprayed.

PUMP-TOP THERMOS: When your baby is newborn, you will need clean, warm water on the changing table for any number of other reasons. Probably the biggest one is that your doctor may not want you to use commercial baby wipes on your baby's sensitive diaper area until he is at least several weeks old. If this is the case, you'll find yourself running back and forth to the bathroom at all kinds of crazy hours to fill a bowl with warm water so you can clean your baby's bottom properly with a cloth or tissue. Not only is this a pain, it's messy and the water gets pretty icky during even one change. An insulated carafe filled daily with fresh, warm water (never hot) solves this problem and then some. If you can find one with a pump top (Thermos brand makes an affordable two-quart model; check their

Web site), even better, since you can dispense clean water with one hand as you go.

DRY WIPES OF SOME SORT: If you aren't using premoistened wipes from the start, you'll have to wipe baby's bum with something (a wet cleaning is really only necessary when you're dealing with a poopy diaper. Too much wiping and washing can irritate her skin). Tissues deteriorate rapidly when wet. Cotton balls are small and messy. Many Girlfriends simply designate a bunch of baby washcloths for the job and rinse them after each use. Others have used squares of soft flannel—tear up old pajamas or buy some cheap flannel at a fabric store. Those of us who can't be bothered with that task have done pretty well with water-soaked squares of paper towel. (Remember—dab and pat clean, don't wipe.) The most compulsive among us use disposable dry wipes, which are sold at medical supply stores or Internet sites. Johnson & Johnson makes some nice-sized, affordable ones called Chix (not to be confused with Chux, which are adult underpads).

WET WIPES: You may not be using these in the beginning, but it's good to have a box or two on hand. When you buy, don't assume all wipes are the same. Some are surprisingly rough to the touch; the fluid they're soaked in can irritate and even sting an infant's skin. Go for a fragrance-free, alcohol-free variety and avoid bargain brands early on.

DIAPER BALM: The big diaper balm decision breaks down like this: You'll either apply it every time you clean your baby's diaper area **or** only when he has an irritation. The Girlfriends have gone both routes and have found that a lot depends upon your baby's individual skin sensitivity and plain old luck. We think the best tactic is to follow your pediatrician's advice, then kvetch to him when you have a problem. Either way, you'll want to have at least one tube of balm for each changing area in your house, as well as for your diaper bag (we'll discuss that later). Which balm to choose? The basic choices are petrolatum-based ointments, such as Vaseline and the original formula A&D ointment, or the white creamy variety, like Balmex and Desitin, which generally have zinc oxide in them. For daily maintenance and soothing mild irritations, each of the balms has its loyal Girlfriend following. In that light, we say, start out with a balm that's affordable and easy to get. If it doesn't do the job, switch to a different overall formulation—for example, if you have no luck with original A&D, go to a zinc-oxide-based brand like Balmex, and vice versa.

ALCOHOL: Keep a small bottle on the changing table for starters. You'll need it to swab your baby's umbilical stump. When you're at the hospital, filch as many alcohol towelettes as you can—use these for stump cleaning until you run out. Some Girlfriends just go and buy additional alcohol wipes—after the stump falls off, they're great for on-the-go first aid.

COTTON SWABS: Dip these in the alcohol; they make cleaning the umbilical stump easier. Don't use swabs in your baby's ears or near any other orifice. Ever.

MISCELLANEOUS OTHER STUFF: Some of the basic hygiene items you'll want to keep on the changing table early on include ointments and dressing for your baby's circumcision wound (if applicable), a rectal thermometer, pacifiers, nail clippers, moisturizer, etc. We will discuss all of these items in more detail in an upcoming chapter.

A Diaper Pail

Practically to a one, the Girlfriends received the same fancy diaper pail as a baby present or shower gift. The idea was that if you put a dirty disposable diaper into the top part of this two-foot high gizmo and gave a little twist, the stinky diaper would be hermetically sealed in its own little pocket of special scented plastic and stored in the base of the pail. The problem was that when you ran out of special scented plastic you had to go out and buy a new "refill" specially designed for the diaper pail and then figure out how to install it. Not to mention that there was also a whole science to emptying the darned thing. Life is too short and new parents have enough to figure out. We all failed to see the magic in this legendary diaper pail and shelved the thing within three weeks.

If you want to use a special diaper pail for disposables, go for a model that uses standard trash bags. The Diaper Champ, though somewhat bulky, is a good bet and really seems to do a good job of sealing off the smell. If you can't be bothered, do what most of us end up doing with kids 2, 3, and 4. Use a small kitchen trash can with a lid and empty it every day. Or just grab the offending dirty diaper on your way downstairs or down the hall and toss the smelly thing into a trash can you keep outside near the back door. (You'll probably go this last route once your child's a toddler anyway, since the poop will really stink, the diapers get scarily big, and you won't want your little hooligan getting into the trash.) If you plan to use a cloth diaper service, the company you choose will most likely provide you with a babyproof diaper pail specially designed for this purpose.

Diapers

While we've hardly spared you our opinion on other matters, we're not going to weigh in on the cloth vs. disposable diaper debate. Depending on your priorities, and your conclusions about which approach is actually better for the world and for your baby, that decision, dear Girlfriend, will be all yours.

IF YOU INTEND TO GO THE CLOTH ROUTE, you should sign on with a diaper service about a month before your due date. (Unless you intend to wash all those poopy diapers yourself. In which case, we'd like to bow down and kiss the hem of your garment. But we don't have much to contribute since few among us has gone this route for any length of time.) The diaper service will drop off your first batch in advance so you have it at the ready. Most services provide a diaper pail and liners, too. You will simply place dirty diapers in the lined pail as you go. Once a week, you'll leave the bag of dirty diapers out for the diaper service, and they will exchange them for a clean set. You'll probably also want to rent or purchase diaper covers from the diaper service or elsewhere. These make cloth diapers a breeze to use—in many cases, you'll simply secure a prefolded, flat cloth inside the diaper cover, slip the whole shebang onto your baby, and Velcro it closed. No need for pins or diaper folding. You might even look into the newer all-in-one cloth diapers—they're generally more expensive but really do simplify the whole process.

IF YOU CHOOSE TO USE DISPOSABLES, start off with one of the big-name brands. You're better off experimenting with generics and smaller brands down the line, when your baby's poop isn't as runny, his skin isn't so sensitive, and you won't be as rattled if a little diaper rash action occurs. Do we have an opinion about which major brand you should start off with? As far as we're concerned, it's the one that's most readily available at the warehouse or discount store nearest you. Should you go for the big brands' basic model or their "premium" variety? Our philosophy in general is to start with what's reputable, most affordable, and again, most available. If your baby starts having rash or leakage issues with the basic model, then you might try moving up the ranks to see if special features, like higher absorbancy or aloe-enhanced liners, help solve the problem. Some Girlfriends claim some brands fit better than others, depending on whether your babe is chunky, scrawny, a wiggler, or a waddler. For fear of sparking a national debate, we'll let you experiment and come to your own conclusions.

HOW MANY DIAPERS SHOULD YOU HAVE ON HAND TO START? During those first clockless days and nights of your newborn's life, you will change his diaper about 100 times every week. Yes—that's right. Newborns feed ten to twelve times a day and food leaves their body about as often. Because their skin is so delicate, you'll have to whisk those diapers off at the merest hint of wetness. Build in some margin for mishaps, like putting on a new diaper, only to hear rumbling down below, and you can see why you'll need to keep lots of diapers on hand.

If you are going to use a diaper service, they will have a very good idea of how many diapers you will need. Even so, you should keep a box of size 1 disposables on hand for emergencies. If you will be using disposables full time, you'll need a nice stash but don't hit the wholesale club yet. Your baby will quickly grow out of the first size, and you'll want to be sure you like the brand of diaper you've chosen. If newborn-size diapers are available, pick up about 100 of these—they have a convenient cutout for your baby's umbilical cord. In addition, buy 100 size 1 diapers. Should you run out of the newborn size before the umbilical stump falls off, you'll move on to the size 1s and simply fold down the top to expose the pretty little stump until it finally dries up and takes a bow. If newborn diapers aren't easily available, don't sweat it. Buy 200 size 1s and fold the top down to expose the stump as we've described.

What to Skip/What's Irrelevant

WIPE WARMERS: A cold wipe can be a rude awakening for a tiny hiney. Especially during a middle-of-the-night diaper change. That's the thinking behind these popular little gizmos. Indeed, there might be something to it. But we've simply raised too many babies without the use of wipe warmers to believe they are a must for proper development. We've also heard about wipe warmer recalls and don't know how necessary it is to keep an electric, heat-generating gadget going all day and all night long in our baby's nursery. Are we going to get all worked up about this? No. If someone gives you a wipe warmer as a gift, make sure it hasn't been recalled (who knows who might be regifting) and give it a go. Should you go out and spend your money on a wipe warmer though? We say nah. If you're worried about chilling your baby's butt, simply scrunch up the wipe in your warm hand before applying it to his sweet, sacred skin.

BABY POWDER: This old-time favorite isn't all that effective in the diaper-care department. Early on, in fact, using powder period is a no-no, since breathing the stuff in can irritate a young baby's lungs.

The Diaper Bag: Mom's Own M*A*S*H Unit

Your most elaborate satellite changing station—for the first year, at least—will be the one you lug around with you. Like your other changing stations, the diaper bag is by no means limited to diaper duties. It should be stocked with basic essentials that will give you your best shot at damage control without returning from the field to mission control. It is the new parent's equivalent of a M*A*S*H unit.

FIRST STEP: SELECT THE DIAPER BAG ITSELF. We'll tell you right off that you'll probably end up with at least two. A large one that will carry your entire arsenal of goodies when you first start becoming mobile with your babe. And a small one you'll grab on your way out to dinner or to your next-door neighbor's. Eventually, you will end up carrying the small one most of the time (or simply stuffing a couple of diapers and a bottle in your own purse) and packing the biggie for all-day outings and quick overnights at Grandma's.

FEATURES TO LOOK FOR: The buzz over the past several years is that a diaper bag should look rugged and cool enough so Dad will feel comfortable carrying it. Well, excuse us, but—hardy, har, har. The cold truth is that you, the mommy, will be the one lugging baby's stuff around most of the time, and you deserve to have a bag that makes *you* feel good and *you* look cool. If, in your opinion, that happens to be a rucksack that makes you look like you're headed for the Australian Outback, then goody for Dad, too. If, however, you're drawn to a snazzy leopard-print number or an elegant black microfiber satchel with gold closures, go for it. Dad will just have to be secure with his manhood, suck it up on occasion, and schlepp anyway. Of course, he also could buy his own diaper bag. (Don't mind us while we fall on the floor laughing.) As far as utility goes, look for a bag that's lined with waterproof material, plenty roomy, and won't show dirt or stains too easily. The changing pad should be generously sized. Make sure the bag is easy and comfortable to carry—if you'll be doing any significant amount of carriage or stroller pushing, we strongly suggest that you carry a backpack-style bag. (Otherwise, the strap of your bag will forever be dropping off your shoulder into the crook of your elbow and driving you crazy.) Compartments are nice, but there's no reason to get carried away. The Girlfriends have all been sucked into buying those ultra-efficient-looking-thought-of-everything diaper bags at one time or another, and we've all eventually given up trying to put things where they supposedly belonged and basically stuffed things wherever we could. Features we've actually used include slots for bottles, a small mesh zipper compartment for pacifiers and nipples, another zippered compartment inside the bag for your keys, wallet, and cell phone, and a section to hold diapers and diapering paraphernalia. A dirty-duds bag is nice, but don't pay extra for it—a Ziploc or a plastic grocery bag will do the job just fine.

CAN WE SUGGEST SOME BRANDS? Baby superstores sell an okay selection of diaper bags, ranging from the puffy Winnie the Pooh variety to mass-market knockoffs of the more sophisticated designer bags. You'll find the coolest stuff by far on-line and in the catalogs. On the rugged, no-nonsense end of the spectrum, Lands' End's bags—which come in a range of sizes and shapes—are winners. If you crave some fashion action, there's no end to the opportunities you'll have to blow cash since all types of big names—from Kenneth Cole to Prada, Kate Spade to Coach—are in on the diaper bag scene. Log onto Babystyle (*www.babystyle.com*) for an idea of the more stylish options out there. Belly Basics (*www.*

bellybasics.com) and Mobile Moms (*www.mobilemoms.com*) both also make nice-looking, smartly designed bags.

THE GIRLFRIENDS LIST: WHAT GOES INSIDE A DIAPER BAG

Backup one-piece playsuit or stretchie

Backup onesie

Receiving blanket

Cloth diaper

Wipes in a Ziploc or portable wipes container

Diapers

Diaper balm

2 resealable plastic bags

Bottle

Pacifier

Rattle / teether

Formula (if applicable)

Infant acetaminophen

A couple of Band-Aids

Sunblock (after baby is six months old)

Cell phone

Wallet

Keys

Emergency contacts and phone numbers

Water for Mom

Antiseptic gel for handwashing

Clean T-shirt for Mom / Dad

Acetaminophen for Mom

Your Auxiliary Diaper Bag:

If you own a car, you should keep some kind of bag filled with changing essentials in the back. At minimum this should include a full change of clothes, several diapers, a tub of wipes, paper towels, first-aid basics, and several small bottled waters.

Should a diaper bag double as a purse?

In theory, it really shouldn't. The chances are high that you will let down your guard, leave the bag untended, and allow some

jerk to slip in and steal your wallet or the whole
But in reality, most of us Girlfriends couldn't i
purse and a diaper bag. Our arms are full er
treat our diaper bag with the same vigilance w.
and never carry anything irreplacable—like our baby's lovey—
inside.

Diaper Rash Redux

Some babies glide through diaperhood with nary a splotch nor a hint of rash on their precious bottoms. Others wage an ongoing battle, regardless of how efficient and valiant their mom's and dad's diaper-changing offensives are. Chances are, your little angel's diaper rash experience will fall somewhere in between these extremes. Here are tools and tricks to keep in mind if and when the scourge should strike:

1. **Use a Spray Bottle.** When a baby has diaper rash, even the gentlest wipes can irritate and sting her skin. In fact, wiping her diaper area period can be bad news—especially if her skin is broken. Our Girlfriend Katy—whose first son suffered through an entire year of diarrhea-ravaged skin and second son had antibiotic-associated yeast infections for years—drummed up this beloved Girlfriend alternative. When your baby has a rash and his diaper area absolutely must be cleaned, lay him on his back, lift his legs, and spritz off most of the mess with a water-filled spray bottle. It's gentle, it's easy, and if you keep a cloth diaper on top of the changing pad as we've recommended, it will handily absorb the water that drips off. (You'll have to undress your baby in most cases, or at least pull his clothes way behind him to avoid

getting them wet. It's inconvenient, but when your baby is in pain, it's worth the effort.) When you're done spraying, gently pat your baby's bum dry. If there is ointment or balm still remaining, there's no need to clean it off. *Note: You can usually find small, empty spray bottles in the hair-care section of your local pharmacy or beauty-supply store. Don't use any spray bottle that has previously held anything other than water.*

2. **Try Adult Under Pads.** When your baby has diaper rash, it's best to let his diaper area air out for a while before putting a diaper back on. This can be a messy proposition, however, especially if the cause of your baby's rash is diarrhea. A good solution: Put your little guy down on an adult "under pad," or "o.b. pad," those disposable absorbent squares that hospital personnel usually put under leaky surgical patients (including new moms). Many of us finagled our initial supply from our maternity ward nurse; fortifications can be found in the adult diaper section of your pharmacy.

3. **Switch to a More Serious Salve.** We think the basic diaper balms do an okay job protecting the diaper area and soothing mild irritations. But we've found other products more effective when it comes to real diaper rash. Top on our list is Aquaphor, a mild, petrolatum-based barrier ointment that's sometimes used on the diaper area of premature infants. (Aquaphor is also great for soothing patches of dry skin elsewhere on your baby's and your own body.) This ointment is available at most pharmacies, though usually not in the baby-care section. Ask the pharmacist, since it is sometimes kept behind his counter.

4. **Try Maalox.** Yes, you can have some, too. But we're really talking about using Maalox on your baby's butt if his rash is caused by diarrhea (get your doctor's permission first). The strange fact is that the very same ingredient in regular-strength Maalox that neutralizes acid in the stomach will act as a diarrhea-neutralizing barrier on your baby's skin. How to do it? Pour the watery portion off of a bottle of regular-strength Maalox, leaving the thick, powdery glop on the bottom. Then use a cotton ball to apply a generous layer of the Maalox to baby's air-dried diaper area. Allow the Maalox to dry before rediapering. Alternatively, you can follow The Children's Hospital of Denver's recipe for "Aqualox": Place six tablespoons of Aquaphor in the bowl of a KitchenAid mixer equipped with the paddle attachment. With the mixer on medium-low, very, very gradually add 6 tablespoons of well-shaken regular-strength Maalox to the bowl. Continue mixing until the ointment is uniformly dispersed—this may take several minutes. (You can actually mix up any amount, just remember that the ratio is one part Aquaphor to one part Maalox.) Apply a thick layer of Aqualox to your baby's clean, dry skin after every bowel movement until his diarrhea has ended and his rash has healed. Stored in a well-sealed jar, Aqualox will keep for up to six months.

5. **Loosen up on the diaper front.** When you put the diaper on, fasten it lightly on your baby so air has the best chance to circulate. Alternatively, you can use a larger size diaper. You might even poke a few holes on the outside of the diaper to increase air circulation. (If you do this, don't leave the diaper exposed, since an older baby may be able to tear off

pieces of the cover and possibly ingest it.) You may have to face some leakage, but hey, them's the breaks. At the first signs of trouble, some of us have also found it helpful switching to diapers that have a lubricated, and thus less irritating, inner lining.

6. **Call your pediatrician.** If a rash doesn't go away after a day or two, regardless of the measures you have taken, call your pediatrician. It may sound alarmist and you may feel silly doing so, but during those first few months of parenthood, this is correct and expected behavior. Your doc may want you to come in or may simply ask you to describe the rash over the phone. If what you see is a red, blotchy irritation, with satellite splotches and perhaps some yellow pustules, the doc will probably tell you it's a yeast infection. In that case, traditional diaper rash creams won't do squat to resolve the problem, no matter how much you apply. A prescription antifungal cream will begin zapping those nasty yeasty beasts almost the instant you begin to apply it. (Nystatin is a favored prescription for young infants; over-the-counter antifungals like Lotrimin can be used—with your doctor's permission—further down the road.) Your doc may also recommend that you apply a bit of hydrocortisone cream or ointment to take down swelling if there is any.

CHAPTER FIVE

On a Roll: The Lowdown on Strollers and Other Wheeled Wonders

Searching for the perfect stroller is a lot like searching for the perfect man. You believe there must be one amazing candidate that will meet all your needs. A well-rounded, dashing sort that can dance gracefully through the world's most sophisticated cities, yet hold its own in the rugged outdoors. A grounded, sturdy type that celebrates the comforts of home and hearth, yet can hop on a plane with élan. Your dream match is solid to the core, yet will never weigh you down. Knows how to stretch a buck, but never comes off as cheap. Can have fun with the kids, but puts their safety and well-being first. Isn't flashy, but always looks sharp.

Yeah. Well, there's no stroller like that, either. Stroller makers have done their darnedest to drum up such a specimen. And they've come pretty close in recent years, we have to admit. However, the Girlfriends still aren't convinced that "one baby, one stroller" is a wise or realistic goal to seek. Experience has shown us that a stroller—or any product for that matter—that tries to do too many things ends up doing nothing particularly well. This usually lands a parent right back in the store searching for a more satisfying set of wheels to fit their needs.

Save yourself some frustration right off the bat and surrender to the idea that you will probably wind up committing to more than one stroller. You should also be prepared to spend some bucks (or have a gift giver or group of gift givers do it), since you generally get what you pay for in this department. Strollers take a lot of punishment and have lots of moving parts. Your baby will be safe in a JPMA-certified bargain-brand model. But if you use yours a lot, you can pretty much count on replacing it a few times during your childrearing years. As our Girlfriend Felicia's nana used to say, "Cheap is expensive."

When to buy:

Give yourself ample time to do your research. Start by sussing out what other mothers are pushing in your neighborhood and perusing opinion sites on the Internet. You'll then be well ahead of the game when you actually head into the stores for a test-drive, somewhere around your seventh or eighth month. If you are doing the buying, don't even worry about joggers and light-weight strollers while you're pregnant, since they generally aren't intended for very young infants. You'll be better off waiting to see what your needs will actually be further down the road. If you are *registering*, however, and you *think* you are going to want a stroller or a jogger for later use, you could do a little homework and put something down on your list. If you get what you registered for, you can return the item upon receipt and earmark the credit for later on.

Where to buy:

Discount and general merchandise stores primarily sell lower-priced American-made strollers, with an occasional sampling of models made by higher-end manufacturers. Baby superstores sell a combination of modest and high-end strollers and carriages, while juvenile furniture and specialty stores are where you'll find the widest array of models from higher-end companies, including certain makes you won't generally find at mass merchandisers—such as Maclaren and Martinelli (the latter of which is basically just a gussied-up Peg Perego). Jogging and all-terrain strollers of varying quality can be found at many of the above; athletic-quality joggers can also be found at sporting-goods stores and bicycle shops. As long as you have the opportunity to test-drive a stroller, carriage, or jogger yourself—either at a local retailer or at your Girlfriend's house—you might consider buying over the Internet. On-line retailers not only offer some of the best deals on wheels—they carry specialty brands you may not be able to hunt down locally.

What's Out There

The first thing you need to do is build your vocabulary. Here are your basic options:

Prams

Oozing old-fashioned European elegance, these big-wheeled buggies are what Princes William and Harry were probably pushed around in. Sometimes called "carriage systems," prams often consist of a metal chassis that has interchangeable components up top, such as a bassinet or a stroller seat. Pneumatic tires or foam wheels, luxurious padding, and excellent suspension provide one seriously comfy outdoor ride for babies—but prams are also bulky, heavy, awkward to use indoors, and expensive.

IS IT WORTH HAVING ONE? A pram is by no means a necessary piece of equipment. However, if someone wants to lend you a pram that's in good shape and you have room for it, you might take her up on it. It can double as an extra "crib on wheels" in your house. A few Girlfriends, in fact, have used the bassinet feature of a pram as their baby's first little crib (most can be fully removed from the chassis and placed on the floor), as well as a sort of "port-a-crib" while traveling.

CAN YOU RECOMMEND SOME BRANDS? There aren't that many players. The brands you'll most likely run into are Inglesina, Peg Perego, and Simo—all of which make a nice, pricey product.

Carriage/Strollers

These can be nearly as large, luxurious, and expensive as prams or scaled back to relatively sane proportions. Traditionally, what distinguishes them from a straightforward stroller is that they recline "fully" (which technically, these days, means about 170 degrees), provide a cozier, more enclosed space, and allow their passengers to face the person who is pushing them—all of which are preferred features when you have a young baby. A "reversible handle" is usually what then allows you to switch from carriage to stroller mode and eventually face your older infant outward. The comfort quotient is considerable here, but these rigs are generally heavy and bulky. As a result, most parents switch to a lighter stroller once their babies get older and store their carriage/stroller for future offspring and expectant Girlfriends.

IS IT WORTH HAVING ONE? Again, check and see if someone can lend you a carriage/stroller that's in good condition. If no loaners appear on the horizon, we believe there are some good arguments for buying one of these—but not too many for going absolutely overboard with your purchase (other than looking fancy). Our Girlfriend Hannah, for example, lived in New York City when she had her first child. Hannah knew she needed a serious carriage/stroller that would be comfortable for her to push long distances, that could stand up to lots of use, and that could protect her babe from the elements, especially on those cold winter days walking to and from daycare. She chose a moderate-sized Peg Perego carriage/stroller and couldn't be more thrilled. It was scaled down enough to function well as a stroller when Gabriel got a little older, and Hannah could fold it up and carry it when she had to. When she needed to use public transportation early on, Hannah simply strapped Gabriel onto her chest in a soft, front carrier and left the carriage/stroller at home. Later she invested in a good lightweight stroller and stashed her carriage/stroller away for her next baby (it ultimately saw her through all three children). In general, if your lifestyle *requires* a lot of walking—especially if your baby is born during the chillier months—we think buying a well-made, scaled-back carriage/stroller may be worthwhile.

CAN YOU RECOMMEND SOME BRANDS? Big American companies like Graco and Evenflo make affordable carriage/strollers with lots of bells and whistles like snack trays and roomy storage baskets. Unfortunately the Girlfriends have found them to be heavy, clunky, and not very durable. We think these are a good option if you won't be putting tons of wear and tear on them. If you're like Hannah and need a fine machine, however, your best bet is to look to the Italians. Peg Perego's carriage/strollers are the gold standard.

Luxury strollers

In their latest attempt to deliver the ultimate do-it-all stroller, manufacturers have taken high-quality lightweight stroller frames and loaded them up with many of the features that were once only found on full-blown carriage/strollers. These bonuses include fully reclining seats, thicker padding and better back support, bigger, shock-absorbing wheels, generous sun canopies, and in some cases, infant car seat compatability. The end result is a slightly heavier stroller that can accommodate younger babies.

IS IT WORTH HAVING ONE? Indeed, this concept comes close to doing every*thing*. But it still won't be right for every*one*. With those extra pounds added on, luxury strollers won't serve mobile moms and dads of slightly older babies as well as their true featherweight counterparts can (with the exception of Combi's version, which we describe below). Nor will they provide the level of comfort and protection true carriage/strollers do for newborns. Before you spend big bucks on these hybrids, think carefully about how you will use yours and if there are more affordable, and perhaps more efficient, alternatives. The heavier luxury lightweights are probably best for suburban Girlfriends who do lots of driving, shopping, and strolling, and want wheels that will be comfortable for their babes to sit in for longish periods.

CAN YOU RECOMMEND SOME BRANDS? A few of Peg Perego's lightweight strollers have the aforementioned features, along with some added pounds and a nice big price. Many Girlfriends have had very good luck with these; some have complained that they don't hold up as well as they should, considering their cost. Combi's pricey luxury stroller is packed with amazing features, including a generous canopy, a fully reclining, padded seat, and pretty good storage features. Sweetening the Combi even more: Their luxury lightweight allows you to snap your own infant car seat right on top of it and face your baby "carriage" style. This is a huge advantage over traditional "travel systems" because you can match the stroller you like with the car seat you prefer, rather than being stuck with the often mediocre components that come in the manufacturer's "4 in 1" or "3 in 1" package. What's astounding is that with all these features, Combi's luxury stroller still weighs in at a mere ten pounds—not much more than some bare-bones umbrella strollers. (Some Girlfriends are put off by the fact that Combi's luxury lightweights don't seem very sturdy. This is generally a function of their featherweight, as opposed to shoddy, design.) Zooper's rugged, luxury strollers get high marks and also hold a wide array of infant car seats. American manufacturers have gotten into the luxury stroller fray—of these, Graco's are the most impressive contenders. Though the Girlfriends haven't generally found these to be as durable as some of their high-end competition, the "luxury" Graco strollers deliver many of the features that matter most while maintaining a light price.

Lightweight Strollers

There are basically two types of lightweight strollers—super cheap, bare-bones contraptions that weigh just a hair more than many newborn babies, and pricey, bare-bones contraptions that weigh about the same or a bit more. The former are virtually disposable, with generally flimsy little wheels, a simple sling for a seat, and plastic hook-shaped handles which give them an umbrella-like look when they are folded. The latter are seriously sophisticated aluminum rigs, with turn-on-a-dime wheels and quick-fold mechanisms.

IS IT WORTH GETTING ONE? We're fans of both for very different reasons. First, it's important to remember that these lightweight strollers don't generally recline extensively, if at all, and often don't offer much in the way of padding or support, so they aren't really suitable for babies under about six months of age. Most Girlfriends started getting regular use out of their lightweights when their babes were somewhere between eight and twelve months old. The high-end lightweights, in our opinion, are the workhorse of choice for errand runners, travelers, and just about any parent who will have her baby in and out of the stroller on a regular basis. They can be folded and unfolded in a blink, tossed into and out of any number of places, and in many cases stand right up to all that punishment. As far as the cheapo "umbrellas" go, we like to stash them in all kinds of places—in the back of each car, at each grandparent's home. You never know when a spare set of wheels might save the day—like when you drive ninety minutes to the Aquarium, only to find your toddler sound asleep in his car seat. Cheapo "umbrellas" are also good for theme parks and other places that require leaving empty strollers unattended for longish stints, since they're so inexpensive you won't be devastated if yours is stolen or damaged.

CAN YOU RECOMMEND SOME BRANDS? The high-end gold standard is the Maclaren, a lightweight most-often aluminum vehicle that practically owns the New York City sidewalks. Serious road warriors can't say enough good things about Maclaren's super sturdy, rugged wheeled, and relatively lightweight Techno model. If that's too costly, even Maclaren's most basic model may very well see you through several children. Combi's feature-packed luxury lightweight (described above) is so light it qualifies as a contender in this category, too. If that model's too dear, you can get Combi's lightweight "sport utility" stroller for under $50. Granted, it's not our idea of a great sport rig. But we're throwing it in here anyway because it packs nice, knobby wheels, multiple recline positions, and a canopy into a neat ten-pound package. On the quasi-disposable side of the spectrum, opt for a model that has the JPMA certification seal, making double sure it has a wide-enough wheel base so it won't tip, and an absence of sharp edges.

Travel Systems

Back in the 1990s, many of us Girlfriends were swept off our swollen feet by the idea that we could get our carriage, our stroller, and our car seat wrapped up in one pushable package. We waited with baited breath to see what future travel systems might include—a mini-fridge? A microwave? Hot and cold running water? After a bunch of months pushing the weight of the world around with us, however, we were less enchanted, especially since the separate components turned out to be mediocre at best. Lately, fancy European manufacturers like Peg Perego have joined the travel system party. Their strollers are lighter and better, but it's going to take some time for them to prove themselves in the car-seat department.

IS IT WORTH GETTING ONE? We just don't see the point of buying a whole system when you can opt for a car seat stroller frame (or a

Combi or Zooper luxury stroller) that is designed to accept most any infant car seat you choose for your child. As we point out in the car-seat chapter of the book, choosing the right car seat for your vehicle and your baby takes precedence over almost all other baby product purchases.

CAN YOU RECOMMEND SOME BRANDS? Graco's lightweight travel system is probably the best of the brood, since their luxury lightweight stroller is pretty good and Graco makes an excellent infant car seat. Peg Perego's travel system includes their well-designed stroller, but Pam the Safety Zealot warns that the car seat it comes with has been problematic.

Car Seat Stroller Frames

Can you say "brilliant"? These frames on wheels can turn most any infant car seat into an instant stroller. They have a nice big storage basket on bottom to boot.

IS IT WORTH GETTING ONE? True to our conviction that simple and specific is best, we think this is one savvy purchase. For many of us Girlfriends, a car-seat stroller frame actually served as our baby's first mode of transport. With a fleece car seat cover-up enclosing the car seat itself, the setup was virtually as cozy as any carriage could be. We then put the money we saved toward a high-quality lightweight stroller or convenient extras, like a jogging stroller. These are a great idea if you have space considerations or if too much paraphernalia will send you over the edge. Our urban Girlfriend Melissa also points out that car seat stroller frames help solve the car-seat dilemma faced by parents who take a lot of taxis: Since the car seat is part of the stroller setup, you won't have to schlep it separately or be tempted to let your baby ride unrestrained. (This is at least true until your baby grows out of his infant seat. God knows what the best solution is after that.) Before you buy, it's important to recognize that car-seat stroller frames are very basic. Since they don't have much in the way of suspension, they probably won't meet your needs if you will be doing extensive amounts of walking on terrain that is rough or bumpy.

CAN YOU RECOMMEND SOME BRANDS? Baby Trend's Snap-N-Go was the original in this category and does a great job. Kolcraft's version isn't a bad choice, either. Note: Car-seat stroller frames work with many, but not necessarily all, types of infant car seats. Check to make sure your components are compatible before you buy or register.

Jogging Strollers

True jogging strollers generally have lightweight aluminum frames, sling-style seats, and large, fixed bicycle-style wheels that help them coast along roads and over rugged terrain.

IS IT WORTH HAVING ONE? If jogging strollers had only been suitable for jogging, they wouldn't have gained the Girlfriend following that they initially did. The same design that made them great for athletes also made it easy for mortal moms to breeze easily over all kinds of irregular terrain—grassy playing fields, buckled sidewalks, and beaches, to give a few examples. We simply had to accept the fact that the sling-style seat didn't recline significantly or provide much support, which meant we couldn't use the jogger until our kids were at least a few months old. Nowadays, with the outstanding sport-utility strollers that are on the market, there's no real need to make a true jogging stroller fill any role other than what was originally intended—that is, as an honest-to-goodness running and power-walking rig for Girl-friends who mean business.

CAN YOU RECOMMEND SOME BRANDS? Baby Jogger II is the original jog-ging stroller and is a great choice for real runners. It's got a light-weight aluminum frame, puncture-resistant tires, a hand-operated brake, and is built to boogie. You can buy a model with smaller wheels for simply getting around, but it's the larger wheels that are really meant for running or rough terrain. A slightly more baby-friendly alternative: Our Colorado Girlfriend Cindy, a structural engineer who spends a whole lot of time on unpaved terrain with her son Sam, raves about her BOB sport-utility stroller. She's com-pared it with her running buddy's Baby Jogger II and feels that it's worth pushing BOB's slightly higher weight since it has better sus-pension, better sun protection, and a more comfortable, reclining seat. Recently, Baby Jogger came out with Baby Jogger 3, which has a reclining seat and shock absorbers. We'll let you know what we think.

Sport-utility strollers

Oversize, knobby wheels or bicycle-style tires give these strollers some of the same rough-going advantages of jogging strollers. The big plus: Many have reclining, padded seats and shock-absorbing suspensions that make them appropriate for young babies.

IS IT WORTH GETTING ONE: If you live in a place with rough terrain or buckled sidewalks, a sport utility stroller may be a very smart option. But don't simply surrender to what's in style like so many of us did with SUVs and buy one of these because it looks cool. Those big, fixed wheels take up room—even when the stroller is folded—and they will drive you bonkers in tight spaces.

CAN YOU RECOMMEND SOME BRANDS? Lots of the cheaper models out there are big on fashion, but not on function. One very decent option, however, is Baby Trend's basic "jogging" stroller. Its heavyish steel frame makes it less than ideal for serious running. But it has a padded, reclinable seat, large pneumatic wheels, and an irresistible price tag. On the high end, the BOB sport-utility stroller mentioned above can also fit into this category. The Girlfriends are also impressed with the rugged rollers made by Zooper. Designed for walking, as opposed to running, these heavyish beauties come with your choice of three or four, twelve-inch pneumatic wheels. Their very infant-friendly features include a fully reclining, nicely padded seat; a rain cover; a mesh sunshade; a full boot (the detachable cover that goes over your baby's lower half); an attachment bar that accommodates most infant car seats; and a reversible seat that allows your babe to face toward or away from you.

Doubles

Twin carriages and strollers come in two varieties: side-by-side or front and back (the latter are known as tandems). Triples and up have all kinds of interesting configurations—but we're not going to venture into that area. (Nor are we getting into the older/younger sibling transport issue—forgive us, but we have to draw the line somewhere, or we will finish this book after our grandchildren are born.)

IS IT WORTH GETTING ONE? If you're expecting twins, you will need to buy a double. The $100,000 question is which variety. Girlfriends with twins say they generally prefer side-by-sides, since both seats can be fully reclined and they provide an equally good view of the world for both children. Side-by-sides are also easier to push outside than tandems, but as you might guess, they are tougher to get through doors and aisles. Several Girlfriends with twins say they ended up buying two single strollers in addition to the doubles. They used the singles whenever two pushing people were available because they were much more nimble and created less of a spectacle.

CAN YOU RECOMMEND SOME BRANDS? Carriages and strollers for multiples are a big investment. Graco makes serviceable, well-priced side-by-sides; Peg Perego makes the hardiest of the bunch. For comprehensive stroller tips and reviews from parents of multiples, check out *www.twinslist.org*.

Here's the Approach

Which of the above will you need when, if at all? There is no "one-size-fits-all" answer. A lot depends on where you live and what your lifestyle is like: what time of year your baby is born; and how much storage space you have. Here's the stroller-purchasing strategy the Girlfriends recommend:

1. **Focus on immediate needs.** As we said above, don't try to solve all stroller scenarios at once. Don't worry about what you'll be pushing later on. Think about what will serve your needs during your baby's first few months and buy what will do the job efficiently and affordably. Some Girlfriends have held off on buying a formal set of wheels altogether at first and used a front carrier like the Baby Björn to tote their newborns around. It freed up their hands and kept their little ones cozy and warm; with the

addition of a lightweight stroller frame, like the Snap-N-Go for their infant car seat, they were really in business.

2. **Check out what other neighborhood parents are pushing.** Not so much to see what's in fashion (and boy, strollers can be a major fashion statement in some parts), but to focus on what's being used where you live from a practical standpoint, with regard to weather, terrain, space, etc. Ask your friends what they have, what they like or don't like, and why.

3. **Fine-tune the features.** Once you determine what basic category you're going for (pram, carriage, stroller, etc.), zero in on brands that have the features you want at the price you can afford (check our "Features that Matter" section). Gizmos that look clever or impressive aren't always what matter most. For example, cheaper stroller brands pack on mom-pleasers like cup holders and toy bars—perhaps to draw attention away from their less-sophisticated overall construction. Do your best to look beyond this stuff. You can buy a cup holder separately for a few bucks if you want one. Even if you don't, not having a spot for your Diet Coke will never drive you as crazy as a bum wheel or a faulty fold mechanism.

4. **Take hubby for a test drive.** Check out options on your own first, but before you buy, make sure the stroller is a breeze for Dad to use, too. Adjustable handles help accommodate parents of different heights, but this feature alone is not a guarantee of a good fit. If one of you is particularly tall, the handles on a particular stroller may not extend enough. Tall parents should also make sure the overall stroller design works for their longer stride.

5. **Buy it and try it.** Or add the winning item to your registry or wish list. If you end up hating it or find it's not what you need—don't suffer needlessly. Return it and try something else.

Features That Matter

1. **Five-point harness.** It's the safest way to secure your child in the stroller.

2. **Nearly Full Recline.** You'll hear the phrase *full recline* a lot when you're shopping for a newborn carriage or stroller. The fact is, new carriages don't actually go to a full 180 degrees, since the experts now think a bit of head elevation reduces choking risks (we're talking phlegm and spit-up here—not Life Savers, Sister). A recline of 170° is considered the ideal for newborns, and that's what you should be looking for. Once a baby is six months old, you can all do very well with a stroller that has a maximum recline of 145°.

3. **An easy-fold mechanism.** Try folding and unfolding the stroller several times right in the store—you should be able to do it without struggling (or a degree from MIT). A "one-handed" fold mechanism is easiest of all, but not a necessity.

4. **Lightweight:** How light, of course, depends on what kind of stroller you will be buying and your lifestyle. Cheaper strollers (with the exception of really cheap umbrella strollers) are usually heavier because they are made with steel and plastic, rather than pricey, featherweight aluminum. You need not go to extremes, but in general, the

lighter the better. Remember—as time goes on, your baby will only get heavier!

5. **Detachable Napper Bar:** If you choose to buy a stroller with a little bar that goes in front of your baby (many folks think it's an important safety advantage), make sure that little bar is removable. Otherwise, when your baby gets older and heavier, you will still be stuck lifting him in and out of the carriage yourself, as opposed to allowing your child to exit the seat on his own once you have undone his harness.

6. **The Right Wheels for Your Needs.** Flimsy plastic wheels deliver a bumpy ride, can jam, break, and generally drive everyone nuts. If you are investing in anything that you will use with any frequency, pay attention in this area. All-purpose carriages and strollers should have front wheels that can swivel freely for good maneuverability, as well as lock in place for easy, straightforward jaunts. Larger, knobby wheels deliver a smoother ride over rough terrain, but they are also bulky and hard to navigate within tight spaces. Choose according to your specific needs. Any carriage you buy should have some kind of brake system, be it on the wheels or on the handle—but don't count on brakes alone. Never leave your child unattended in his stroller for this—and many other—reasons.

7. **Decent storage baskets.** This is no minor matter, considering that you'll be schlepping all of baby's as well as your own stuff, and one or both of your arms will be busy pushing the stroller itself. The problem is (go figure) that many of the priciest, best-functioning strollers on the market

have relatively puny storage baskets. Some strollers that cost hundreds don't even come with a basket—you actually have to pay extra for the "luxury." On the flip side, many of the less expensive, less sophisticated strollers and carriages have baskets so big they could practically transport another child. (Though in some cases, they are nearly impossible to get to when the stroller seat is fully reclined.) Your decision here depends upon your lifestyle. In general Girlfriends who have needed to depend heavily on a stroller or carriage for getting around have been happier buying better-made equipment and compensating for the less-than-ideal storage situation. Our tactics have included forgoing a satchel for a backpack-style diaper bag, which allows you to carry a bigger load more comfortably, frees up both arms, and makes pushing easier. We've also attached net stroller bags to the handles—but beware of overloading these because the weight can tip a stroller backward. Fortunately, this tends to happen when you remove your baby from the stroller, since the child's weight is no longer counter-balancing what's on back. It's a pain nonetheless, and could be dangerous if your child is very light.

Stroller Accessories

STAY-WARM STROLLER BAG: These are like little sleeping bags that strap onto your stroller, walker, or jogger. They provide better coverage than a simple blanket with the big bonus that they will not fall off and get caught in the wheels. These bags are generally intended for babies six months and up and are big enough to last through the toddler years. A couple of brands to consider: The lightweight fleece Cozy Rosie, one size fits most strollers and joggers (*www.cozyrosie.com*); the Toastie Toddler, one size fits most strollers and joggers and is available in thick fleece and weatherproof styles (*www.mobilemoms.com*); and the rough-and-tough Buggy Bag from cold Canada, which comes in a stroller or jogger style, in your choice of lightweight or heavy-duty weatherproof materials. (*www.buggybag.com*). When push comes to shove, of course, a standard stroller blanket will do if you don't want to be bothered with clever accessories.

HEAD AND BODY SUPPORT PAD: These pads are often marketed as car-seat accessories. Child passenger safety experts flat out warn against using them in this capacity because they can interfere with a car seat's performance in the event of a crash. Here's a smarter idea: Beef up the cushioning, neck and body support on a lightweight or luxury stroller by threading the pad onto the stroller harness. Our Girlfriend Shane found this item provided particularly wonderful support and coziness for her preemie daughter Lucy. A handful of manufacturers make these pads, including Infantino. Again, this ain't a necessity for most babies, but should the need arise . . .

RAIN SHIELD: If a rain shield doesn't come with your stroller or carriage, ask a salesperson to recommend one that will fit. Urban dwellers really give these a workout.

BUG NETTING: A fine mesh net helps protect summer babes from mosquitoes and other pests. Ask a salesperson what will fit your rig.

ADDITIONAL SUNSHADE: If you want to beef up the sun protection provided by your stroller's canopy (if it has one), there are numerous clip-on stroller umbrellas and sunshades specifically designed for the job. The Girlfriends particularly like an Australian-made shade called Pepeny. It ties on in a jiff, provides protection from UVA and UVB rays, and folds up into a pocket-size packet. You can find it at specialty stores and on-line (*www.pepeny.com*).

CHAPTER SIX

Feeding

G o ahead, breathe a big sigh of relief. We're going to. Because this chapter is not going to get into the whole breast vs. bottle issue. This is a little book with a lot of opinions about straightforward baby stuff. The merits of breast- or bottle-feeding are a whole 'nother can of worms, and there are any number of books and busybodies that can deluge you with opinions on the subject when you're ready for it. (Come to think of it, they may not even wait for you to be ready.) Just in case you think the Girlfriends are bailing on you when the going gets sticky: We've actually devoted a chapter to this issue in *The Girlfriends' Guide to Surviving the First Year of Motherhood*, where we do our best to shine some light on common considerations that may help you reach your decision. Should you never pick up a copy (which we find hard to imagine), we'll tell you now that the Girlfriends don't sanction or endorse any particular feeding method. We are unanimous in our belief that a mother's job is to feed her baby good, healthy food. The particulars are up to you, Girl-friend, and don't let anyone tell you otherwise. Now let's talk about what you'll need to feed.

Breastfeeding Essentials

WHERE TO BUY: These days, high-quality breast pumps and other nursing supplies are widely available, thanks to baby superstores and the Internet. In many cases you can buy or rent a pump right at the hospital where you deliver. Also keep in mind smaller breastfeeding boutiques and individual vendors for your nursing needs. (A lactation consultant or a local La Leche representative can probably tell you if there is such a thing or person in your area.) These folks may not always have the best prices, but they tend to be extremely knowledgeable about nursing and may even let you try professional samples before you buy. Breastfeeding specialty shops also act as a magnet for other nursing moms, which can provide an important sense of community and cama-raderie for you, especially during those early months.

WHEN TO BUY: Buy or register for most of your nursing parapher-nalia in advance. The big exception: your breast pump. More on that on page 138.

What You'll Need:

GOOD SUPPORT AND ADVICE. Having a like-minded person or three to answer your questions, unabashedly grab your engorged breast and try to help your baby latch on to it, or show you how to work an intimidating-looking breast pump can make all the difference in the world when you're just getting started. So a good circle of support is your Number 1 breastfeeding acquisition. Find out from your local hospital if there's a nursing mothers' group in your area. Track down the name of a lactation consultant or two. (Contact the International Lactation Consultant Association, 919-787-5181 or log on at *www.ilca.org*; your hospital or pediatrician should also be able to provide names.) Briefly chat with these folks to make sure you're comfortable with their personality and philosophy about breastfeeding. When you give birth, demand an appointment with the hospital's in-house lactation consultant and leave with her business card in your bag (if you like her). Last but not least, turn to a veteran Girlfriend breastfeeder for encouragement and advice. We're the ones who will come running when the phone rings at all hours—to show you what we did to relieve a plugged duct or simply boost your confidence by confirming that your baby does not in any way look like he is starving to death.

READING MATERIALS. Even with a supportive army at the ready, you'll be happy to have dependable written resources as close as your bedside, handbag, or desktop. Pick up a good breastfeeding book—*The Nursing Mother's Companion* (Kathleen Huggins) and *Nursing Your Baby* (Karen Pryor, Gale Pryor) are both informative and nonpreachy; La Leche League's *The Womanly Art of Breastfeeding* (Gwen Gotsch, Judy Torgus) has a strong point of view but is a classic nonetheless. And bookmark key Web sites on your computer—La Leche League's technical information and advice is solid; Medela, one of the top manufacturers of breastfeeding supplies, also runs an excellent site, *www.medela.com*.

NURSING BRAS: Let's talk about those nursing bras. Yes, your breasts are going to continue growing throughout your pregnancy. But we're talking inches at most, not exponents. Thereof, those of us who bought our nursing bras during the seventh or eighth month of our pregnancies found that the size we chose was pretty much on the mark for our future needs. We had the added bonus of using these nursing bras as maternity bras during our third trimester. Start out with two and don't skimp on the time you spend finding a style that fits your body. (A poorly designed bra can make nursing inconvenient and can even trigger a breast infection.) It's ideal if you can buy your first bras at a maternity or nursing specialty shop or perhaps a department store so someone can fit you professionally. (Don't be shy about letting this lady get right in there—in a few months you'll guffaw at the fact that you ever considered your breasts private property.) Once you start nursing and determine if you like or dislike the bras you've chosen, you can fine-tune your bra supply.

Features and brands to look for:

In general, it's best to avoid nursing bras with an underwire, since the pressure of the underwire may cause your milk ducts to become blocked. Girlfriends with very large breasts who feel they need "underwire-type" support have had good luck with Playtex nursing bras, which have a flexible fabric "braid" built in to do the job. (If you turn out to be so gigantically huge that you will fall to the floor without the help of an underwire, consult a lactation consultant about what to get and how to minimize your risk of complications.) Stretchy bras that simply allow you to pop your breast out are becoming popular, and several Girlfriends like them, but lactation consultants are concerned that the pressure of the elastic when it is pulled aside may irritate the breast tissue. As for traditional flap-style nursing bras, be sure to examine the "flap" mechanism and choose one that is easy for you to manage with one hand. In general, the Girlfriends have found that snaps are easier than hooks and eyes but they can sometimes pop open more easily. Flaps that unfasten from the top are more convenient than the flaps that unfasten from the center. Our favorite all-around nursing bra has to be the Bravado! (that exclamation point is part of the name, not an indication of overexcitement on our part). Its cotton/spandex fabric and sports-bra back provide a superbly comfy, supportive, and flexible fit that accommodates your changing breast size; the nursing flaps provide maximum breast exposure for easy access, and it comes in a range of cool colors and patterns. Leading Lady is another good brand and is favored by lactation experts since it's made from 100 percent cotton. If you wind up using a Medela electric pump, you might want to consider buying their nursing bra and accessory kit that allow you to essentially hook up to the machinery and pump hands-free. Yes, this takes the Elsie factor up yet another notch, but once you spend some time pumping, you'll realize what a boon hands-free can be.

NURSING PILLOW: You might want this accessory early on when your baby is small and you have no clue about what you're doing or how to hold him. (A few months down the road, you'll be able to nurse just about anywhere in just about any position without anything to help. We're talking about standing up in restaurant bathrooms, sitting through Saturday matinees, and of course—lying down, sound asleep. Just wait. You'll see.) A classic choice here is a crescent-shaped pillow called the Boppy—it can double as an all-purpose propper for your baby before he can sit on his own. But the Girlfriends' favorite by far is something called My Brest Friend. Yes, your husband will make fun of the name. You'll probably laugh when you first use it, since the whole thing kind of wraps around your body and Velcros at the back, making you look like a lunch counter. But this thing rocks—that "wrap-at-the-back" feature provides much needed back support and the pillow's shape provides a perfect platform for your baby. There's even a little pocket on My Brest Friend for your TV remote, lanolin, gum, shot glass (just kidding), or whatever little items you consider indispensable. If you are having twins, check out the Anna Pillow (*www.annaproducts.com*). The large-size version easily accommodates two babies for nursing as well as bottle-feeding; the adjustable design facilitates correct latch on and makes the pillow very comfortable to use.

NURSING CHAIR AND STOOL: Every Queen deserves her rightful throne. See our "nursery" chapter for ample justification.

A BREAST PUMP: Just about every mom who plans to nurse will need some way to draw milk out of her breast other than attaching a baby to it. Sure, you might hear that it's possible to "manually express" if necessary. But take it from Girlfriends who have attempted this feat in certain moments of desperation (like when your breast is too engorged for baby to latch on), manual expression is pretty much on par with hand-plucking your own bikini hairs on the old comfort meter. The only thing that's worse is watching helplessly as your breasts balloon like the Hindenburg, then waiting for them to burst into flames. (Or at least develop mastitis, which is probably more painful.)

The catch here is that it's hard to know what you will need or what will work for you until you are actually in nursing mode. You may develop a complication early on and need to rent a hospital-grade, high-power machine. You may only end up needing a manual pump for occasional pumping so you can go out to dinner or relieve engorgement. You may decide to buy a high-quality portable electric so you can pump at the office. Then again, you might choose to bag nursing altogether just three days after you return home from the hospital. The best approach: Think about what your needs might be for each scenario and have a retailer in mind. You or your designee can then get the goods when the occasion arises.

As far as brands and models go, our suggestions are as follows: If you decide to pump only occasionally, your best choice by a long shot is the Isis manual pump made by Avent. It may look innocuous—the gizmo twists right on to an Avent bottle. It may only weigh a couple of ounces. It may work so silently you can't believe it's doing anything. But believe us—the job it will do extracting milk will be close to miraculous. Several Saturday-night pumpers among the Girlfriends have used their Isis as their one-and-only pump. Even those of us who have invested in portable electrics have gotten lots of use out of our tiny, feather-light Isis. Our Girlfriend Kim toted hers to a Bruce Springsteen concert and pumped and dumped in the ladies' room while the Boss belted out "Born to Run."

Should you turn out to have significant pumping needs, don't spend your time or money on a cheap model made by any old baby product manufacturer. We haven't met a pumper yet who did so and was truly happy with her decision. Here's what we suggest:

- Renting a hospital-grade pump has been the best option for Girlfriends with nursing complications or those of us who weren't quite sure how long we intended to nurse but wanted the ability to store significant amounts of milk. Medela—which pretty much owns this market—provides a national listing of places that rent their pumps on a short- or long-term basis, *www.medela.com*.

- If you decide to return to a full-time job and continue nursing, it's probably worth investing in a piston-powered, portable electric breast pump. In this department, there are really just two names worth considering: Medela and Ameda Egnell. Both are highly effective and have convenient features—check them each out to see which best suits your needs.

NIPPLE SALVE: Massaging your own breast milk into your nipples is fine for daily upkeep and soothing minor irritation. But if your poor nipples get so raw and cracked that even a gentle breeze makes you howl like a banshee, you'll need something more. Don't be tempted by health-food folks who tell you to use Vitamin E or similar oils—they can irritate your skin. Check with your doc first, of course, but we feel a good bet is probably pure, medical-grade lanolin—it can be soothing and may actually speed the healing process along. (If wool sweaters make you itch, avoid lanolin. You may be allergic.) Lots of companies sell lanolin intended for this purpose—the Girlfriends like Lansinoh, since it's widely available and fairly priced. Buy just one 2-ounce tube, since a little goes a long, long way. Aquaphor is another good choice and is actually preferred by dermatologists—it contains a small amount of lanolin but is less allergenic.

NURSING PADS: These are designed to fit inside your nursing bra and absorb leaks. In general the Girlfriends prefer the disposables to the reusable cotton kind because they are more convenient and more absorbent. (If you have very sensitive skin, go with cloth pads.) Start off with a small quantity of whatever brand is readily available and does not have a plastic lining (nonbreathable plastic can actually irritate the breast). Don't get carried away, however, since not all moms leak, and even if you do, it may only last until your supply regulates itself. A Girlfriend may even pass along her surplus disposable pads. If you end up spouting like Old Faithful, you may want to look into the nursing pad picture a little further. There are some good disposable options out there—Lansinoh pads are particularly nice, since they have an adhesive strip that helps keep them in position, as well as a pinkish hue and a thin, contoured shape, which makes them less obvious under your clothes. If you're a light leaker, you can bag commercial pads altogether, cut circles out of old white T-shirts, and just stick 'em inside your bra. Wash them in the machine and toss 'em out when they get icky.

FOUR 4-OUNCE PLASTIC BOTTLES: See below for details.

2 SILICONE NEWBORN-SIZE NIPPLES. See page 143 for details.

BOTTLE BRUSH: See page 143 for details.

EMERGENCY FORMULA: You never know when some unplanned event might prevent you from nursing. Keep a few small cans or bottles of ready-made or dry formula on hand just in case. The hospital, no doubt, will also send you home with some in your formula-company-sponsored goody bag. Do confer with your pediatrician in case he or she has specific recommendations.

What You May Need:

Since not every nursing mom will require the following items, buy them on an as-needed basis:

BREAST SHELLS: You might consider using these if your nipples become extremely sore or raw. They essentially create a protective bubble over the area and allow air to circulate and speed the healing process. (Should you find yourself in such a situation, you may very well want to contact your lactation consultant or pediatrician first to determine what the cause of the problem is and how it should best be treated.) Medela makes a nice product called Soft Shells that look relatively inconspicuous. Under your clothes, that is. BTW: Breast shells are sometimes also recommended predelivery if you have flat or inverted nipples.

BREAST MILK STORAGE BAGS: You can use regular bottles to freeze breast milk. But they take up a lot of room and hog up bottles you could use for feeding. Storage bags are the obvious alternative. Don't try to make do with anything but high-quality pouches designed specifically for the job (Medela's are good). Our Girlfriend Tula tried to use disposable plastic bottle liners and found them difficult to seal shut and she spilled some precious breast milk in the process. She cried. You might, too.

Hitting the Bottle:
What You'll Need To Bottle-Feed

WHERE TO BUY: Any place that has good prices and is convenient—Kmart, baby superstores, your local CVS, you name it.

WHEN TO BUY: Anytime before your baby is born.

What you'll need

6 PLASTIC BOTTLES: Sorry, but we just can't get all gushy about those expensive, "scientifically designed" baby bottles that seem to be the rage. Why spend all that money when your baby may do very well with the three-for-five-bucks variety? We say start with bottles that are affordable and easy to find—Evenflo's three-pack is a good basic choice. You can buy them in the four-ounce size—or just go for the eight-ouncers, fill them half way, and keep the bottle well tipped to prevent air from getting in. Then you'll have room to grow when baby's appetite does. If your baby doesn't like what you're offering him or if he seems to have gas problems, then experiment with different bottles and nipples. We say avoid doughnut-shaped bottles in general. They look like a good idea, but they're tricky to clean. Though some Girlfriends are fans of disposable bottles, like Playtex, most of us find the systems expensive and more of a pain than a plus, but to each her own.

2 SILICONE NEWBORN NIPPLES: If the bottles you buy come with brown latex nipples, it's not a bad idea to replace them with the clear, silicone variety in the slowest-flowing newborn size. Slow flow is important early on to prevent gagging; if you are breastfeeding, it's also important because when milk comes out from a bottle nipple too easily a nursing baby may not want to bother working for the relative trickle that comes from mom. We recommend silicone because it won't degrade like latex will—an important point if you are tossing your nipples in the dishwasher. (Bottle nipples, of course.) You'll ultimately need to have more nipples on hand, but start with just a couple, since you'll have to see if your baby likes what you've selected. Whether you go with a straight nipple for starters or the orthodontic style with the little bulge at the tip is up to you—simply make sure that what you select is very slow flow, compatible with the bottles you've selected and—this is important—easy to find. Once baby gets used to one type, you'll have a hard time convincing him to switch his loyalties.

BOTTLE BRUSH: Buy one of these even if you'll be washing your bottles in the dishwasher. Sometimes bottles get gunked up and only a hand scrub will help. Sometimes you may run out of clean bottles before the dishwasher is ready to run. Choose a bottle brush that has a nipple brush on one end—the little thing does a gentle yet thorough job.

DRYING RACK: Even if you put your bottles in the dishwasher, you'll need a place for them to hang out and dry completely. Those cheapo plastic bottle racks do an adequate job, but they can take up precious counter space. Our Girlfriend Shelly found a space-saving alternative in the earth-friendly Seventh Generation catalog (*www.seventhgen.com*). Their plastic bag dryer consists of a round pedestal from which several wooden spokes jut up and out. Shelly used it to dry bottles early on; she now gets extra use out of her toddlers' resealable plastic snack bags by rinsing them and hanging them to dry—just like those eco-types intended. Other Girlfriends have let their bottles air-dry on the dish rack and called it a day.

Formula

This is going to involve some decision-making. Here's our approach.

FIRST, CHOOSE THE BASIC FORMULATION. Actually, this part is easy, since you should put the decision in your pediatrician's court. Your general options will include milk-based, soy-based, and predigested varieties. You'll also probably be advised to use formula that is iron-fortified.

SECOND, CHOOSE A FORM. Formula generally comes ready to use, in liquid concentrate, or as a powder. The ready-to-use is by far the most expensive option, with powder being the most affordable. Yes, there are Girlfriends who are more than happy to spend extra bucks for premixed convenience. The fact that premixed formula now comes in recloseable milk-jug type containers makes life even duckier for this contingent. The more pragmatic among us simply aren't convinced. We not only think it's nuts to spend so much money on such a long-term commitment; premixed formula also takes up a lot of space and it spoils if you open a container and fail to use all of it within a short window of time (this is a particular consideration for breast-feeders who are supplementing). Powdered formula's nearly ready nature does take a bit more effort, but it also turns out to be one of powder's greatest advantages. Moms on the move can simply fill a bottle with clean water, head out, and add formula powder whenever they want—there's no need to refrigerate or heat the thing. For added convenience, you can purchase single-serving sleeves of powdered formula or little dispensers that hold the right amount of formula in individual compartments. There are even dry-formula bottles that keep the water and formula separate until you're ready to mix them. At home you can mix up a pitcher and decant formula into bottles or make each one individually. It's really not a big deal. We're sure we've gotten quite a number of Girlfriends grouchy with this strong point of view, but hey, if you didn't want opinions you wouldn't be reading this book. *Note: Until your baby is 6 months old, your doc might want you to sterilize the water you use to make formula. If so, heat a pot of water in the a.m., boil for one minute, let it cool, then decant it into bottles or a pitcher.*

THIRD, CHOOSE A BRAND. Nutritionally, the major brands are pretty much the same. Your decision should be determined by which you can get most easily in the form you want and at the best possible price. (Your pediatrician may also have a strong opinion for some reason.) Since warehouse stores are an ideal place to buy formula, you may want to pop by, see what they're selling, and base your decision on that. Don't buy your first installment of formula at the wholesale club, however—if your baby doesn't like it or it doesn't agree with him, you'll be stuck with a warehouse-size surplus. Start with the small container of the type you're considering (you may even want to check if your doc has a sample), then move on to the wholesale club if you don't have a problem. *Note: Just in case you're wondering why you need to commit to any one brand and one form—formula varieties may be similar nutritionally, but each does seem to have its own particular taste and consistency. Babies get accustomed to what you give them—which can make switching dicey.*

What You Might Need:

DISHWASHER BASKET: If you'll be washing bottles in a dishwasher, you'll need one of these for your collars, bottles, and nipples. You'll use it down the road for sippy-cup components and other small items.

DRY FORMULA DISPENSER: This handy plastic decanter will hold several premeasured servings of dried formula. When you need to feed on the road, you can just open the top and dump the perfect amount of powder into your water-filled baby bottle. Tiny Love and Munchkin are among the companies that have made these gadgets.

FILTERED WATER PITCHER: Unless you have water purity problems where you live (or a baby with a compromised immune system), there's probably no real need to boil your water before mixing it with dry formula. (But check with your doc, of course.) If you aren't quite comfortable with taking cool water straight from the tap, consider buying one of those Brita pitchers that comes with a built-in filter. Who knows if it will really protect your child from anything, but it will make you feel better. Fill the Brita several times throughout the day and keep it on the kitchen counter so you have tepid water at the ready when you need it.

COVERED PITCHER: If you use dry formula exclusively, you may want to mix up a pitcher of the stuff each morning instead of preparing individual bottles. Some pitchers, often called "formula pitchers" or "stirring pitchers," have a built-in paddle and crank which allow you to mix up the formula easily before you decant it. They can be tricky to find—check some of the baby gear catalogs or key in "stirring pitchers" on your Internet search engine.

SMALL THERMOS: See sidebar on Warm Heart, Cold Formula.

What You Probably Won't Need In Either Case

BOTTLE WARMER: Breast milk should not be warmed in a microwave. Something very mysterious apparently happens to it. (Does it turn into diet Coke? Eggnog? We can't tell you, because we've all been too terrified to experiment. Or at least too terrified to admit we have.) So if you'll be pumping and storing, you'll basically have two reheating options. The bottle giver can warm the bottle in hot (not boiling) water while the baby cries. Or he can heat it in a bottle warmer while the baby cries. We just don't see any real advantage of the latter over the former. So skip spending the extra bucks.

Warm Heart, Cold Formula

Call us hard-hearted, but unless formula is coming ice cold from the fridge, we can't see any reason to heat your baby's bottle at all. The key is not getting him used to this in the first place. Should you be dealing with really cold *formula*, it's fine to warm it very briefly in the microwave. You'll simply have to be very careful to shake the bottle thoroughly to eliminate hot spots and test it before you give it to your baby. A convenient tip for nighttime feedings: Keep a water-filled baby bottle by your bedside and just dump in a premeasured amount of dry formula when your little angel starts howling for food. Our Girlfriend Shane kept a stash of single serving premix in the nursery for the very same purpose. If you just can't bear the idea of giving your baby tepid formula—*and you're using dry formula*—fill a small thermos with warm water and bring it to bed with you. You then won't have to make any middle-of-the-night trips to the kitchen. You'll also be able to tuck the thermos into your diaper bag for feedings on the go.

STERILIZER: The party line among most pediatricians and lactation consultants these days is that unless you have a premature or immune-compromised baby, you do not need to sterilize your bottles and other feeding equipment on a regular basis. Even if you do need or choose to sterilize, the Girlfriends just don't see the big deal about tossing the stuff in a pot of boiling water, as opposed to sticking it in one of those fancy sterilizers. After an initial boiling in this style, it's okay to wash your breast pump components and bottle paraphernalia on the top rack of your dishwasher. If you don't have a dishwasher, give the stuff a nice scrub with hot water and dish soap and put it out on a dish towel or drying rack. (If you have well water, you may need to sterilize. Check it out with your town and pediatrician.)

What You Should Skip

BOTTLE PROPPERS: Proppers may seem like a nifty convenience, but they're basically bad news. Sticking a bottle in the face of a small person who may not be in the position to push it away can pose a choking hazard. It's also sorta lazy. Feeding should be not just an act of sustenance, but an opportunity for a baby to bond with his caregivers. That's hard to do if he is sitting by himself in a bouncy seat with a bottle propper as his companion. A notable exception: Girlfriends blessed with multiples insist that bottle propping was a necessity at times. If this is your situation, do what you need to do but keep your babies close at hand and watch them carefully.

Breast Pumps: To Borrow or Not to Borrow

Talk about controversy. Some of the Girlfriends have borrowed a breast pump with the same nonchalance they borrowed their bouncy seat. It's a pretty appealing idea, considering how expensive pumps are. It also seems pretty safe, since it's fairly easy to buy a new set of the components that actually come in contact with the breast and breast milk. Then there's the other contingent, like our Girlfriend Caitlin. When a gal pal mentioned to her that she planned to borrow, Caitlin was so revolted by the very concept, it took her ten minutes to lift her chin up off the ground and halt the wave of nausea that rolled over her body. As your dutiful Girlfriends, we've looked into the matter, and here are the facts.

Although breast milk isn't intended to pass through the actual workings of a portable breast pump, it can, in fact, occur if milk gets "backed up" while a person is pumping. If that happens, there is no practical way to decontaminate the pump. This means there is a chance—minuscule as it may be—that pathogens carried in breast milk could be passed on to the baby who drinks it. Considering the fact that these pathogens may include HIV and hepatitis, this is no matter to take lightly. (Rental-grade pumps are designed so they can be completely decontaminated and are thus an entirely different story.) What you're exposing your baby to, then, all comes down to who you're borrowing or buying from—and who else they've lent their pump to. With this in mind, the Girlfriends think the used-breast-pump concept is one potential petri dish to pass up. Yes, a pump might cost you $400. But why take risks when it comes to a baby's very sustenance?

Down The Road: High Chairs and More

We're not going into great detail about solids here. Obviously you'll need some spoons with a soft coating that will be gentle on baby's little mouth. You'll want some plastic bowls and a few plastic-lined bibs. And a hose to wash down the kitchen. What we really want to talk about is the high chair, since it's something you may end up including on your wish list. We're also mentioning a little gizmo we love since you might not know about it unless the Girlfriends clue you in right now.

The Gizmo We Love—The Baby Food Mill:

Even if you buy prepared baby food, you might like having this handy tool close at hand. It's a tiny, dishwasher-safe, portable mill with a crank handle that quickly purees any relatively soft food—bananas, peaches, cooked pasta, cooked veggies, cooked meats—and makes it suitable for your baby. Kidco currently makes the only one we know of—if you can't find it locally or in one of the baby-gear catalogs (the latter won't necessarily identify the food mill by its brand name), check Kidco's Web site, *www.kidcoinc.com*, for stores.

The High Chair

The high chair started out as a pretty basic piece of gear that served a pretty basic purpose: holding your young child in place so you can feed him. Now, of course, you can buy high chairs that can do just about everything. The new wave of high chairs can roll. They fold up. They recline. They have extra trays. And they can be darned expensive. Are we saying that all these features are just plain stupid and a total waste of money? Absolutely not. For our apartment-dwelling Girlfriend Melissa, a nice compact fold made it possible for her to have a high chair without selling the family sofa to make space for it. A reclining seat makes it possible for your youngish babe to hang out at your level while you eat dinner—as opposed to on the floor in a bouncer seat or infant car seat. (Note: Do not feed a baby in the reclined position due to the risk of choking.)

FEATURES TO LOOK FOR: Take a few minutes to think about the features you're really going to use. Don't get sucked in by mere possibilities. Talk to Girlfriends with similar living situations who are one or two years out with their babies and see if they really, truly roll their chair around as much as they thought they would. Did they use all those adjustable heights or did they simply switch to a booster seat when baby was ready to join the family dinner table? In the Girlfriends' opinion here's what features really count when it comes to high chairs:

JPMA CERTIFICATION: High chairs have been associated with numerous injuries and deaths, often due to flawed design. The industry has developed safety standards to reduce risk, but meeting them, believe it or not, is voluntary. The JPMA seal will tell you that the new high chair you are buying has the basic features necessary to help keep your child safe. These include a tip-resistant design; a safety harness with crotch strap; a crotch post that comes between your baby's legs and keeps him from slipping out from under the tray; and a locking mechanism that prevents the high chair from folding unexpectedly. None of them will be worth much, however, if you yourself aren't vigilant. Always use the safety harness when your baby is in the chair and never leave your baby unattended while he is in it.

A LARGE TRAY THAT CAN BE REMOVED EASILY WITH ONE HAND: Ideally it should have deep sides and wrap well around your child on either side to minimize mess.

EASY-TO-CLEAN DESIGN: Avoid high chairs with lots of exposed seams and joints. A vinyl seat that can be wiped clean is ideal.

CAN WE SUGGEST SOME BRANDS? In the luxury high-chair world, there are two major players. Peg Perego's Prima Pappa is the Mercedes of high chairs. It's well-built, has all the bells and whistles, and makes you look good. The Chicco Mama is the Lexus—it's well designed, has lots of great features, and makes a swell—if somewhat more subtle—impression. Each has pluses and minuses. On the downside, the Prima Pappa is a bit more expensive than the Mama and some of the Girlfriends found it tricky to clean. On the plus side for Pappa, it folds more compactly than the Mama. The Mama, on the other hand, is roomier than the Pappa and comes assembled (a big deal, believe us). On the downside, some of us have found Mama's tray to be a bit high and too far out for younger babies. Spend some time comparing the two side by side before you make your decision.

THIS IS ASSUMING YOU'RE BENT ON BUYING A BIG-NAME SEAT. Frankly, we just can't get all caught up in the high-chair status circus. We'd save our bucks for a real Mercedes. Many of us have been perfectly happy with Graco's well-priced, easy-to-clean full-featured high chairs. Even the most basic version—and there are many versions—has a reclining seat, adjustable height, and a big tray with one-hand adjust. If you want to get fancy, you can pay more for a model with lockable wheels and an extra tray (though we really can't see the advantage of having two trays to clean instead of one). The main drawback as far as Graco's full-featured high chairs go is that they take up a lot of space. Should you only need a high chair to do the simple job it was originally intended to do, go for Graco's most basic, no-frills high chair. (Be careful about borrowing; there was a recall several years ago.) It's not fancy, but it's very practical and affordable.

Booster Seat for Feeding (Not to be confused with booster seats that go in cars)

Boosters are small seats that strap on to a regular chair and essentially "boost" your older baby so he can sit right at the dinner table with the rest of the family. They are one of the reasons why lots of us have survived very well without fancy adjustable high chairs. Several boosters now come with removable trays, so they can also serve as a mini-high chair. Just be aware that boosters really shouldn't be used from the get-go since they are only suitable for babies who can sit very well on their own. The trays are also pretty dinky and sometimes don't snap on very securely. With that in mind, we think the booster-tray option is fine in a pinch situation, such as when you're traveling or eating at Grandma's, but we don't think it's a substitute for a formal high chair. The First Years makes a sturdy fold-up booster that's relatively easy to clean, since it's dishwasher safe. The tray can be knocked off a bit too easily, though, so it's better to use it right at the table or at least be extra cautious if you've got an active toddler in there. Whatever brand you choose, make sure it has at least three straps: One that goes on your baby, one that goes under the seat of the chair and one that straps around the chair back. Stay away from booster seats that clip right onto a table or counter—they can be difficult to secure correctly and many injuries have been associated with them.

Tip: If your baby appears to be sliding out of position in the high chair when he first starts using it, put a square of thin rubber shelf liner on the seat. It will help give his butt some traction.

Top Ten Signs of A First-Time Mom

10. A surgical mask dispenser at front door and Phisohex offered as the powder room hand soap.

9. Never speaks above a whisper and goes rigid and white if you do. She is convinced that babies need quiet above all else, and that we heathens cannot be relied upon to provide it.

8. Actually puts the crib side up and down to accommodate the baby's installation. Experienced moms learn to live with a little free fall at the end.

7. Inspects the contents of each diaper and writes down notes in a journal. E.g. "Pumpkin-colored poo poo, with little chunks or stringy bits. Smells like cookie dough gone bad or overcooked spinach."

6. Every time she comes over to visit, usually under social duress, she explains that she left the baby at home because "she was napping," no matter what time of day or night it is. If she hears that all four of your kids have sniffles, she says her hellos from the driveway and heads home to shower and gargle before checking on her napper.

5. Sends a mass e-mail to tell you the baby was in the 90th percentile for head circumference at his last pediatrician's checkup.

4. Would happily trade her husband for three nights with the "Baby Whisperer" and never look back.

3. Carries a diaper bag the size of a steamer trunk.

2. Changes her baby's mobile once a week to keep challenging his little mind.

1. Owns the whole library of Baby Einstein and played Mozart for her belly while pregnant.

CHAPTER SEVEN

Arms Relief: Front Carriers, Bouncy Seats, and Other Sanity-Saving Baby Holders

In case you don't know this already, your baby will essentially take over your upper appendages—for that matter, your upper body—for the first year of its life. Of course, you will adapt. You will, in fact, be amazed by how many things you will learn to do with one hand and a small human on your hip. There will be times however, when you will need a break. So you can pee without someone on your lap. So you can take a hot pot off the stove. So you can tie your shoes. Take it from the Girlfriends, it'll be much nicer if your baby isn't crying on the floor or in her crib while you attempt to accomplish these feats. The following items have a shot at providing some short-term amusement. Many folks will tell you that none of them are mandatory. Technically, they may be right. But THESE HAVE KEPT MANY GIRLFRIENDS FROM LIGHTING THEIR OWN HAIR ON FIRE AND RUNNING OUT INTO THE STREET. For that reason, we think that acquiring at least a few of the following is a very good idea.

WHERE TO BUY: First, see what you can borrow. Most of your Girl-friends with older babies and children will be just itching to unload this stuff. If *you're* doing the buying, purchase these items at whatever superstore or discounter has the brand and model you want at the best price. Specialty stores carry this stuff, too, but you'll generally pay more for the somewhat unnecessary lux-ury of fancy fabrics and lavish accessories.

WHEN TO BUY: You won't be able to use some of these things—like the high chair and the stationary exerciser—until your baby is well past the newborn stage. But if you're registering or have eager gift givers, put them down on your wish list if you think you'll want them.

What You'll Need

Front Carrier

A front carrier does exactly what the name infers: It's a little car-rier that allows you to strap your baby onto the front of your body. Very early on, your infant faces inward and enjoys a tanta-lizing view of your breasts and chin. A little later (when he gets some neck control), you turn your baby around so he can face out and take in the rest of the world's breasts and chins. We think—barring preexisting health conditions of yours or your babe's—front carriers are indispensable. Not just because they are a convenient and cozy way to get around town (you can actu-ally wrap your coat right around the front carrier when it's really cold). Not just because they provide easy access to places where carriages may be unsuitable—subway stairs, walking trails, weensy boutiques, and some snooty museums. Front carriers are a godsend because babies tend to be as happy—or happier—in them as they are in your arms. Yet, of course, your arms are blissfully free. The front carrier was the only thing that allowed our Girlfriend Pam to eat a meal with two hands during the first four months of her colicky son Zane's life. On one mildly famous occasion, Pam's husband Paul started to choke on a lamb chop during a neighborhood barbecue. Pam quickly jumped up and began performing the Heimlich maneuver on Paul. There was one minor catch: Pam completely forgot she still had Zane strapped onto her chest. Father and son both fared fine—though the neighbors were a bit traumatized by the spectacle. We guess the moral of the story is—use your front carrier and use it well, but don't get carried away. You obviously don't want to wear it while you're weight lifting, cooking lamb chops, or doing CPR.

CAN WE SUGGEST SOME BRANDS? In the United States, front carriers are often referred to as Snuglis. Snugli is actually not a generic term but a specific brand made by Evenflo. (Kinda like Ziploc or Kleenex.) Snuglis are a fine and relatively inexpensive choice but the Girlfriends think there are better-designed and more comfortable options out there. Our favorite is something called the Baby Björn. It's a little tricky to get on and a bit expensive, but the straps are nice and wide, and provide lots of support for parent and babe alike. *Note: Baby Björn did have a recall several years ago. If you borrow or inherit a Baby Björn, contact the manufacturer since you may need to order a free repair kit to correct the problem.*

ANOTHER OPTION: THE SLING-STYLE CARRIER. These cradle your baby across your body, may be a little easier on your back, and offer the decided benefit of allowing you to nurse discreetly (and virtually hands-free when your baby's a bit bigger). The downside is you can't be quite as active with your baby in the sling as you can be with the Baby Björn. Overall, though, they're a great thing. Nojo makes a sling that's very popular, but it's kind of big and puffy. Model Cindy Crawford shook up the sling scene when she plugged a sleeker alternative made by New Native. Considering the orders that poured into the California company's offices, you'd think Crawford had endorsed a cure for cellulite. Celebrity or not, the New Native is a nice-looking and comfortable cotton sling that comes in a range of sizes and decidely unbabyish hues—including black. It's a superb option for traveling and great to tuck into your diaper bag, since it folds up into almost nothing.

Bouncy Seat

Originally, bouncy seats were a pretty straightforward concept. They consisted of a light metal frame with a gently elevated sling that gave your newborn a somewhat more interesting alternative to lying flat on his back and staring at the cracks in the ceiling. A gentle touch of your hand or foot and the little seat bounced just enough to sooth your baby while you finished drying your hair, folding the laundry, etc. True to form, the baby-gear makers did their best to make a good thing more complicated (and of course, more expensive). They added the toy bar. The sun canopy. The built-in vibrator. The thick cushioning. The option to transform the thing into a mini-rocker. In a matter of years a basic piece of gear mushroomed into a whole new micro-market. The choices on store shelves now are astounding, as are many of the price tags. The Girlfriends have to admit that some of the add-ons are nice—some of us especially love the vibrator. (Get your mind out of the gutter.) But we beg you—don't get carried away with this purchase. The big seats with bells and whistles may look wonderfully comfy, but they aren't as easy to drag around with you, from the kitchen to the den to the bathroom to the yard (which is probably what you'll be doing). And you'll be spending lots of money on an item that has a relatively short window of use.

Note:
Bouncy seats are very portable, and it's very tempting to plop them on all kinds of surfaces. You might see moms put them on top of a table, you might hear some folks rave about the magical effect of placing a bouncy seat on top of a warm, vibrating clothes dryer. Don't even *consider* doing this. Because bouncy seats are so light, they tend to migrate out of position on their own and can also easily be knocked onto the floor. THE ONLY SURFACE A BOUNCY SEAT—OR FOR THAT MATTER, ANY BABY CONTRAPTION—CANNOT FALL OFF OF IS THE FLOOR ITSELF. SO KEEP IT THERE.

CAN WE SUGGEST SOME BRANDS? Compared to the fancy models out there these days, the basic bouncers from Fisher-Price may look a little humble. But they do a fine job and have seen many moms through multiple babies. They have the vibrator (babies hate it or love it), the sun canopy, the toys, plus a restraining belt that unclips from both sides of the seat—something that will make taking your baby in and out far easier. If you are bent on getting an expensive, big-time bouncy seat that can actually double as a second sleep spot and a mini feeding chair, take a look at the one from Combi. It has multiple recline positions, a big canopy, a vibrator, and more. Girlfriends who have it are happy with it.

What You Might Want

BABY SWING. For some of us with fussy or colicky babies, a battery-operated or windup swing was the only thing that kept us from selling our own young. Others among us used our swing a lot simply because our babies got a kick out of it. A healthy handful of Girlfriends banished their swing to the basement after about one week, since the thing seemed to generate screaming as opposed to soothing. (Then, of course, there was Stacy. Her daughter Kate was not only colicky; she hated the swing, too. Stacy wound up driving around the block a lot with the little gal. Prozac also helped—Stacy, that is.) If you are buying all your own stuff, don't get a swing until you have had the chance to actually put your baby in one at a Girlfriend's house or even right at the store and see if he likes it. If you have budget or space issues, go ahead and wait till you are downright desperate. Should you be registering, go ahead and put the swing down on your list. You can always return the swing and earmark the credit.

CAN WE SUGGEST SOME BRANDS? Your best bet is Graco's swing. It's sturdy and the one that most Girlfriends have had experience with. Fisher-Price also makes some good swings—some have an option that allows the baby seat to swing side to side as well as back and forth, which some babies might find more soothing. (Be careful about borrowing, since both brands have had recalls.) If you go for the Graco, you'll have to decide whether to go with a wind-up or battery-operated model. The battery-operated models are more expensive to buy and use, but we think the convenience is worth it. They are also the only Gracos as of yet that have the open top, which makes putting baby in and taking him out much easier. (Visually, the open top makes these swings look less like some horrid, huge contraption is taking over your living room.) When you shop, you'll notice that swings come in many gussied-up styles. None of these frills has impressed us much. Built-in music is tinny and becomes incredibly annoying (to Mom and Dad) after a while. Some swings have oodles of speeds—you'll end up needing three at most. Some have built-in toys—these become invisible after a short time. So we say "Stay basic."

Stationary Exerciser

Stationary exercisers were invented as a safer alternative to walkers, which we discuss in the "skip it" section below. They usually consist of a play tray up top with a rotating, pouchlike-seat for your baby in the center and a round-bottomed "tray" down below which allows your baby to rock and jiggle the whole apparatus by pushing his feet. These circus-hued behemoths dot the lawn of just about every other suburban garage sale. Homeowners can't get rid of these space hogs fast enough—once their babies have grown, that is. But during the early days, stationary exercisers can be sort of nice to have around since they provide a fixed spot where baby can play and generally rabble-rouse. One important point: There has been some hubbub about the fact that babies who spend time in stationary exercisers experience some developmental delays. We buy this as a risk if you are tempted to keep your infant in it for extended periods. But if you are using your stationary exerciser as a way to keep your baby happy and safe in one spot for a short period, it's probably an okay idea. (Still, many of the Girlfriends have passed on this piece of gear altogether since its limited use just doesn't seem worth the risk.) See our "You Can't Be an Idiot" sidebar for more.

CAN WE RECOMMEND SOME BRANDS? Evenflo kicked off the whole stationary exerciser trend with their Exersaucer, and they pretty much still own the market. Now, of course, Evenflo has capitalized on the original. Instead of just a couple of toys, the deluxe models have so many trinkets and gizmos they look like amusement parks. Although this may seem tantalizing, take it from us—whether you have three toys or thirteen built into a baby product, they all eventually become invisible to the baby who is regularly seated in front of them. You're better off buying the basic model and loading up the tray with a variety of funky baby-safe objects. Yes, your little one will toss them all off onto the floor within a handful of minutes. But you won't be leaving him in there for much longer than that, right?

Portable Play Yard

These are "criblike" pieces of gear that pack up relatively easily so your baby has a place to sleep when he's visiting Grandma. Even if you won't be doing a lot of overnights, we think a portable play yard is a great thing to have on hand. As we mentioned elsewhere in the book, if you buy one with a "bassinet" insert, you can use it as baby's first sleeping spot and blow off buying a formal bassinet altogether. A portable play yard is also great to use as a satellite sleeping spot and changing station elsewhere in your house. Several of us kept our play yard in or just outside the kitchen well into our babies' second year of life—it's a perfect place to plop kamikaze crawlers when you have to deal with hot pots and don't want a little person underfoot. Eventually your play yard will become a repository for toys, blankets, and other junk you can't get around to putting away. When the collection nears the top rim of the play yard, it will be a sign that your baby has not been in the thing for a while and it's time to fold it up and put it away. *Note: Play yards have been associated with several deaths; numerous models have been recalled. Typically, victims have pulled up on the sides of a play yard that has not been fully locked into position and the play yard collapsed. Manufacturers have redesigned play yards in order to minimize the possibility of this and other accidents occurring; it's still important, however, that you follow setup instructions exactly and personally show anyone who will be using the play yard (grandparents, baby-sitters) how yours works.*

CAN YOU RECOMMEND SOME BRANDS? We think that Graco's Pack 'N Play is the way to go here. It has lots of great feature options, and, most important, it is very sturdy and has one of the best safety records in the play yard category. The bassinet feature is worth shelling out extra for; we also like the changing-table insert (though the latter is certainly not a necessity, since the bassinet can be used as a changing surface).

Infant Activity Gym

Early on, when your little angel is not being held in some way by someone or something, she will be lying somewhere on her back. An activity gym will make this prospect lots more interesting and pleasant for everyone—for at least five minutes. The basic concept is that the gym dangles toys or entertainment over their prostrate audience. The objects can be ogled at first, batted around a little later. Come to think of it, baby gyms are a fun place in general for you and your baby to hang out together—and they will free up your arms from dangling toys so they can sneak in for a tickle or a squeeze.

CAN YOU RECOMMEND SOME BRANDS? Our favorite baby gym is something called the Gymini. It consists of a colorful, padded mat with two padded, toy-adorned arches that crisscross over it. The real beauty of it is that it folds up flat in seconds, so it's easy to store or take along to Grandma's. There are lots of knockoffs on the market nowadays, and most of them seem just fine.

Baby Backpack

These are sort of like the backpacks that hikers use. But instead of carrying GORP and gear, they're designed to hold little humans. They're great for trail walking and traveling in places where paved roads may not be the rule. If a Girlfriend is willing to loan or bequeath one of these, pounce on it if you think you might have use for it. If you're doing the buying, we think it's important to wait on this purchase, until you really find a need for it. Our Girlfriend Margot, who was a forest ranger in Yellowstone in her salad days, spent big bucks on a high-tech baby backpack long before her baby arrived. It was, in effect, her promise to herself that once she became a mom, she would continue doing the things she loved to do in her customary adventurous style. The reality was that Margot saw the world a whole lot differently once her baby arrived. She was pooped by the time the weekend rolled around—instead of tackling a different peak every Saturday, all she wanted to do was go to Grandma's house in the burbs and get some R&R. After an initial camping vacation in the Adirondacks (where the tent leaked, everyone's clothing got soaked, and the baby ended up wearing a snowsuit the entire time), Margot knuckled under to the idea of a family resort with flush toilets and was a much happier mommy for it. Sure, the backpack got some limited use, but it mostly sat in a closet and just pissed Margot off when she caught sight of the thing. When Margot finally did catch up on her sleep, she found that the hiking and walking she was up for was better suited for a sport-utility stroller than a backpack. All this isn't to say that your experience won't be very different—but why not wait and see how you feel? Also be sure to try on the backpack with your baby on board. There are several different brands and each will fit your—and your partner's—body differently.

CAN YOU RECOMMEND SOME BRANDS? Hardcore mountain moms and dads rave about the baby backpacks made by Madden. They have thick padding for parent and baby, distribute weight extremely well, are very durable, and can carry a child until he weighs about seventy-five pounds (*as if!*). They aren't cheap, though—so it's important to really consider how much use you plan to get out of the pack. Tough Traveler makes a wide range of durable, well-designed baby backpacks—some parents love the way they fit, some find that they don't fit well at all, so be sure to try before you buy. Kelty also makes a range of good baby backpacks that are worth checking out.

What to Skip:

Walker

This "play tray" on wheels has been associated with more injuries than almost any other piece of baby gear. Usually, the injuries have occurred when the walker has careened down a flight of stairs. Manufacturers have tried in recent years to drum up all kinds of safety devices that might reduce this risk. We're not convinced. Unlike some other gear that can have negative effects over time if misused, a walker provides no margin for misuse. Even if you yourself should never turn your back on or allow your walker near steps, there's no guarantee everyone who spends time with your baby in your home will be as vigilant.

CAN YOU RECOMMEND SOME BRANDS: Nope.

Jumper

Jumpers are seats that suspend your baby inside a doorway by some sort of bouncy tether and let them jump their jollies out. If you even mention these contraptions within earshot of Pam the Safety Zealot, she starts hyperventilating. She has pretty good reason for doing so: Jumpers have been associated with a significant number of injuries. There have been several recalls—sometimes due to the coil or spring actually snapping or breaking. Should you have your heart set on having a jumper nonetheless, keep in mind that jumpers aren't compatible with all doorways. This is especially true in older homes and apartments, since their doorways can be unusually high and tend to have funky moldings. Some doorways are simply too narrow for a baby to bounce safely within them. If this ends up being your situation, don't attempt to gerryrig. Return the jumper and find a safer alternative.

CAN YOU RECOMMEND SOME BRANDS: No. We aren't hot on any jumpers. There are better options out there, Girlfriend.

Playpen

Consider the portable play yard your updated substitute—it provides a safe place for you baby to play and is a whole lot more versatile than an old-fashioned playpen.

The "You Can't Be an Idiot" Factor

There are certain baby products that have a greater potential for misuse and negative side effects than others. Stationary exercisers, for example, have been associated with developmental delays in some babies. Swings are jokingly referred to as vegematics.

And yet we've included—and perhaps recommended—some of these items in this chapter. Are we crazy? No—we are Girlfriends who are not underestimating the intelligence and judgment of similarly minded Girlfriend mommies and mommies-to-be. We know that if you buy a stationary exerciser, you will not leave your baby in there for more time than it takes for you to gobble down a ham sandwich. We know that if you buy a swing, your baby will not be abandoned in there for endless hours. To put it bluntly, WE KNOW THAT YOU WILL NOT BE AN IDIOT.

This is assuming that you and your similarly nonidiotic partner will be the only people using the aforementioned items and others like them. If you will have a baby-sitter, or there will be others watching your baby (which would be a healthy thing to do at some point), make clear what your rules are about this gear and set specific limits on how they are to be used.

CHAPTER EIGHT

Bath, Hygiene, and Health Essentials: What Works, What's Just Fancy

Regardless of the fact that babies frequently sit in their own pee and poop and may spit up more than they seem to keep down, they don't need a whole lot of hygiene supplies. They exude their own heaven-sent fragrance that far outshines any man-made perfume on the planet. Their soft (if somewhat pimply) skin generally doesn't require exotic soaps and creams. Their feather-fine hair—if they have any—has no need for deep conditioning.

Nevertheless, you will come across a zillion fancy unguents and potions specifically designed for your precious baby. The pastel packaging will make you sigh audibly in the store. You will turn over your credit card to the clerk and thoroughly overlook the outrageous prices you may be paying. At least that's true on the first couple of occasions you purchase this stuff. Sooner or later, however, reality will set in and you will realize that BABIES ARE A LONG-TERM PROPOSITION AND YOU WILL BE

BATHING AND CLEANING THEM PRETTY DARNED OFTEN. Spending big bucks on esoteric toiletries is just plain silly, so resist temptation. Do use the fancy stuff if someone gives it to you as a gift. But stick by your pragmatic senses when the money is coming from your own wallet and go for the basic baby brands that saw most all of us very safely through babyhood. If your little one turns out to have a skin condition or sensitivity, talk to your pediatrician or a dermatologist about what products might be necessary before you break the bank on boutique concoctions.

As far as healthcare paraphernalia and medications are concerned, you will need to keep certain basics on hand at all times. This, too, will be a pretty short list, since babies—especially very young ones—shouldn't be taking medications, including those that come over the counter, unless it's absolutely necessary. And then, ONLY MEDICATE YOUR BABY WITH YOUR DOCTOR'S PERMISSION. Should you be tempted to down some extra-strength Excedrin or something more interesting yourself (and you will be), get your pediatrician's okay first if you're nursing. Breast milk not only passes on the flavor of last night's Mexican meal to your baby, but many of the medications you take as well.

WHERE TO BUY: Pick up your initial supply of toiletries and medical supplies at the baby superstore where you're buying the rest of your gear, or at a pharmacy. Once it's clear that baby responds well to what you've chosen, buy in bulk at your local warehouse or discount store. (Decant the bulk stuff into the small dispensers from your initial purchases; they'll be a whole lot easier to manage.)

WHEN TO BUY: Buy all of this anytime during your pregnancy. You'll need it in the house when baby comes home from the hospital.

Bath Gear

As we discussed in some detail in the *Girlfriends' Guide to Pregnancy*, babies aren't immediately eligible for a real "bath." Sponge bathing is the rule until the umbilical stump shrivels up and falls off and, if applicable, that circumcised little penis is free of bandages and fully healed. Even at that point, your newborn will hardly be in need of serious scrubbing. As our Girlfriend Helen's mother-in-law snapped when she noticed our Girlfriend practically running for the baby tub mere seconds after Phoebe's stump parted ways with her body, "What's the rush? It's not like that baby has been crawling through the forest." Being hormonally compromised at the time, Helen took offense. But, well, Florence had a point. When you do decide to take on the bathing effort, every other day will be more than adequate. Here's what you may want to have on hand:

BABY BATHTUB. Somehow the Girlfriends are totally comfortable with the thought of putting an older infant in the same tub where mom and dad stand with their athlete's feet. Or putting him in the kitchen sink where we just washed a pile of tuna-casserole-coated dishes. Early on, though, we just like the idea of providing a pristine newborn with his own clean little bathing spot. (There's absolutely no science behind our feelings, so please don't go fretting to your pediatrician.) Besides, giving very young infants a bath is about as easy as maneuvering a greased water balloon. So the smaller, cozier, easier to access, and forgiving the environment, the more secure you'll all feel.

CAN YOU RECOMMEND ANY BRANDS? We're not very picky about any particular brand. The tub you choose should be made of sturdy plastic, with a gently reclined, slip-resistant surface for your baby to rest on. A drainage plug will make emptying the tub easier. It's also nice if the tub isn't too big so that it can fit right into your kitchen sink. Safety First makes a well-priced baby tub that pretty much fits this description. Built-in toys, fancy shampoo caddies, and complicated harnesses are just window dressing; it's really not worth paying extra for them. Also, don't get sucked in by infant/toddler tubs that claim to have features for babies who are ready to sit up on their own. By the time your baby is doing that, you will have gotten over the "ick" factor, and your hearty guy will be happily bathing in the big, fungusy tub like the rest of the family, or, at least, in your kitchen sink.

BABY BATH PAD. If you have no issue whatsoever with putting your newborn straight into a sink or bathtub (and MANY very rational Girlfriends don't), you should put him on one of these. Skip the old-fashioned versions that look like a huge old sponge. The new and much improved variation—Leachco makes one called the Safer Bather—is well contoured, elevates a baby's head nicely, wrings out easily, and dries quickly. Do be sure to fill the bath or sink with only a few inches of water—anything more is dangerous. Besides, some bath pads will start to float, which obviously, isn't the idea here.

BABY WASHCLOTHS. Small and soft, they have a better shot at getting stuff out of a baby's chubby folds and tiny crevices than clunky adult washcloths. Stick with 100 percent cotton; some less expensive brands are made with synthetics, and they don't wear nearly as well.

CLOTH DIAPERS. Can you imagine taking a bath and the water only reaching halfway up your rear end? Chilly thought, huh? Well, that's pretty much what it's like for a young infant when he's bathing, since the water can only be a couple inches deep at most. A simple solution: Thoroughly soak a cloth diaper with warm water from the tub and lay it down the length of your baby's torso. The weight and the warmth will be very comforting for him. The lack of crying will be comforting for you. When the cloth begins to cool, pour more warm water over the cloth with a plastic container (see below).

PLASTIC CONTAINER. You know, like the ones the delis give out when you buy potato salad and coleslaw. The one-pound size is just about right. Use this to scoop up the meager amount of water in the baby bathtub, so you can rinse the soap off your baby's body and otherwise delight him with gentle drizzles.

BATH TOYS. You will not need or want these until later. Earlier on, your baby won't be up to holding anything. And both of *your* hands will be on *him*.

MESH TOY BAG. When your baby switches to the big-boy tub, you will be amazed at the collection of toys and bizarre playthings he amasses. Our Girlfriend Jessie took an inventory at one point when her twins were three and a half. Among the bath booty: 8 naked Barbies, six pieces of Tupperware, a small plastic watering can, 4 Matchbox cars belonging to the boys next door, an egg-beater, a colander, and a metal whisk. A mesh bag that suction-cups to the side of the tub will help you keep track of at least some of the smaller junk. Don't overfill the bag, though, because you'll have a mildew problem. Lots of companies sell these, and they are all pretty mediocre at sticking in place. Should your baby grow up to be a big-time bathtub junk hoarder, you can also take Jessie's approach and simply designate the old infant bath tub as the new storage bin for bath toys.

TOWELS. Use a cute little hooded getup with a duck design or simply grab a grown-up towel off the rack. See our opinions on this in Chapter 2.

Baby Upkeep and Grooming

ALL-IN-ONE BABY BATH SOAP. Technically, you only need warm water and a washcloth to clean a newborn baby's skin. But if you just can't keep yourself from cracking open that bottle of baby bath, no one will swoop in and arrest you. Don't bother buying separate baby shampoo and body soap, however—the all-in-one washes will make your life far simpler. (Truth be told, the Girlfriends were using baby body wash on their babies' hair long before the manufacturers came up with their all-in-one idea. Maybe their all-in-one formula is a bit different, maybe it's just savvy marketing. Who knows.)

Can we recommend some brands? The head-to-toe goods from the big guys like Johnson & Johnson suit us just fine. They're gentle, affordable, and widely available. Try to find the bottles with a pump top—it'll be easier to dispense what's inside. FYI: All the "gentleness" in the world will not prevent a soap or shampoo from irritating your baby's eyes. What generally does the trick in tear-free formulas is a mild anesthetic. Some all-natural baby washes and shampoos out there market themselves as "ultra gentle" and anesthetic free. We've tried some of them—and let us tell you, they are not "tear free" by a long shot. Either these folks have never actually bathed babies or they know something about keeping soap out of little eyes that we don't. As we see it, if anesthetics make baby bathing happier and easier, then bring 'em on.

DIAPER-RASH CREAM/OINTMENT. See "Changing Scene" chapter for strong opinions.

PETROLEUM JELLY. A good all-purpose salve for dry skin patches, chapped noses and lips, and for getting that rectal thermometer in easily. Or at least, more easily. A&D ointment works well here, too.

AQUAPHOR. Similar to petroleum jelly but more effective on trouble spots. Particularly fabulous on diaper rash (see Changing Scene chapter), in the opinon of many Girlfriends.

MILD MOISTURIZER. Generally, newborns don't need lots of help in the moisturizer department. But if you live in a dry climate, like our Colorado Girlfriend Cindy, your baby's skin may end up like parchment paper if you don't anoint him regularly. Whatever the case, it's good to have something that's mild and fragrance-free on hand. No need to buy a baby formulation (though the smell is divine). Ask your pediatrician for a suggestion or try to track down Cetaphil lotion—it's very light, water-soluble, unscented, and doesn't leave a greasy film on the skin. Opt for a bottle with a pump top if you have a choice.

MASSAGE OIL. You can use a bit of lotion while you massage, but a nice oil will make it easier for your hands to glide over that dumpling of a body and generally won't absorb into the skin as quickly. There are all kinds of special baby massage oils on the market, but no real need to buy them (unless doing so is a thrill, which it was for many of us). A little safflower oil from the kitchen will do the job very nicely. If that seems just a bit cannibalistic, pick up a bottle of cold-pressed sweet almond oil from a health food store. If your baby has rashy or delicate skin, check with your pediatrician first.

HAIRBRUSH. There's a good chance your baby won't have any hair to brush when he makes his debut. Keep a small one with firm nylon bristles on hand, however. Should you experience the joy of cradle cap—your baby will look like he has extremely bad dandruff—massaging a bit of oil into his scalp with the brush will help get rid of some of those scales. Eventually, we promise, you will also have some locks to tame.

BABY MANICURE SET. *You* may not have a shot at getting a manicure for a while. But it's a must for your baby—those little nails grow like weeds and they can do some serious scratching. It's easy enough to buy a preassembled kit complete with a baby nail clipper, baby safety scissors, and tiny emery boards (they sometimes include a comb and brush as well). If not, round up the components yourself. You'll want several options on hand because there's simply no way to tell which method will work best and be least terrifying for you. Clippers tend to be quickest, but the wrong squeeze and you'll come away with some flesh, too; you'll also need to file baby's nails after you clip them since the clipper creates sharp edges of its own. Safety scissors (be sure they're blunt-tipped) are slower and clumsier, but a little more forgiving. If you're a total chicken and you can hold your babies hand tightly enough, simply resort to using only the emery board and file away. You'll have an easier time succeeding at any of the above strategies if you attempt them after a bath when baby's nails are soft, and ideally, when he is nursing or asleep.

COTTON BALLS. You may need these for getting gook out of your baby's eyes, and other touchy tasks like wiping the umbilical stump and vaccination spots.

COTTON SWABS. Use these only for cleaning up that umbilical cord stump or applying ointment to your baby's circumcision area or minor cuts and scrapes. Never use swabs near the eyes or ears.

Feel-Better Paraphernalia

RECTAL THERMOMETER. In the past we've recommended using those electronic ear thermometers and skipping rectal thermometers altogether. But the more enthusiastic temperature takers among the Girlfriends have convinced us that rectal is probably the best route to an accurate reading. It's not that ear thermometers are bad—it's just difficult to angle them correctly in a tiny baby ear so you can get an accurate reading. We're not going to cede our ground altogether, however, for the sake of absolute accuracy. Those old-fashioned, mercury-filled glass thermometers may be the gold standard, but they're just too darned scary. A digital version with a flexible tip will get you close enough. Even better—see if you can find a rectal thermometer that's sort of shaped like a plug. Because of the gizmo's cone shape, the pokey part can only go into the anus so far, thus relieving you of any fear—no matter how irrational—that you will push the thermometer too deep and it will come out your baby's belly button. The First Years makes one of these. Whew.

NASAL SYRINGE. If your hospital doesn't send you and the baby home with one of these, you'll need to buy one at the pharmacy. You'll want a nasal syringe on those occasions when you must resort to actually sucking the mucous out of a very congested little nose. Putting saline drops in first will help loosen things up. Look for bulb syringes with a small, tapered tip. Hold the syringe just outside the nostril, press the bulb and release it very quickly for maximum effect. *Note: Use this sparingly and only when necessary. Overuse can irritate an infant's delicate nasal membranes.*

COOL-MIST HUMIDIFIER. You'll need one of these on occasion to help ease your child's—or your own—congested nose and chest. A humidifier will also be vital when you inevitably awaken to the sound of a seal barking and realize that your baby has croup. Don't wait until someone is sick in the middle of February to buy one, though. Chances are, everyone else in town will be under the weather, too, and your local pharmacy will be sold out. Old-fashioned steam vaporizers are not an option when you have small children because they pose a serious burn hazard. That leaves potentially germ-breeding cool mist and the expensive ultrasonic/fluorescent/bacteria killing variety for you to choose from. Ask your pediatrician for his opinion on the subject. The Girlfriends aren't overly thrilled with any of the options but tend to lean toward the basic cool-air models and make a point of cleaning them very frequently. Diluted chlorine is great for the job; just be sure to rinse the humidifier thoroughly with plain water afterward.

2 SILICONE PACIFIERS. In theory, you may think pacifiers are an absolute bane. In reality—when your newborn is shrieking inexplicably for the second straight hour—there's no telling what you'll be willing to try. Keep one orthodontic and one straight pacifier on hand. Your babe might reject one and accept the other. As we've mentioned before, clear silicone is a better nipple choice than the brown latex variety. Of course, some babies never take to pacifiers—think of it as one less habit you'll have to break them of later.

ICE PACKS. Ice packs should never go directly on a baby's delicate skin, so be sure to wrap whatever you use in a towel or cloth. Try to find ice packs that are filled with a gel that stays sort of soft even when it's cold; it'll be a little less offensive to your young victim. You might also consider having on hand a couple of those chemical ice packs that aren't kept in the freezer, but instead get cold when you twist the bag. (Never leave your baby or toddler alone with an ice pack of any kind—the packaging and contents can, in some cases, be a choking and/or poisoning hazard.) Lots of our babies absolutely loved something called the Boo Boo Bunny—it's a freezable plastic ice cube surrounded in part by a plush bunny-shaped cover that makes the thing easy for little hands to hold. Wetting a washcloth or sponge and storing it in the freezer inside a Ziploc bag works well, too.

STERILE GAUZE. Buy a box of mixed sizes. Let's not even think about what you'll need them for.

BAND-AIDS. Keep a box on hand but use them cautiously—Band-Aids and other bandages of their ilk can peel off and pose a potential choking hazard.

TWEEZERS. Keep a pair specifically for splinter removal. Obviously, since the roughest surface your infant will probably touch is your unshaven leg hair, this won't see a lot of action early on. Just you wait.

INFANT-STRENGTH ACETAMINOPHEN. We're talking Tylenol or some generic version of it. You'll need it to relieve fever, teething pain, and other minor ouches. Be aware that there is a huge difference in concentration between the infant strength and children's strength versions; acetaminophen can be toxic if a child is given too high a dosage over time. Be sure you choose the right formulation for your child's age and weight and ask your pediatrician or pharmacist exactly what the dosage should be.

INFANT-STRENGTH IBUPROFEN. Look for Advil, Motrin, or some generic version of them. If your baby's fever does not respond to acetaminophen, your pediatrician may recommend that you try the ibuprofen. Vicki loves Hyland's Teething Tablets, a homeopathic remedy. Check with your doctor before using them, of course.

TEETHING GEL. Most of us have found acetaminophen far more effective in the teething-pain department. Ask your pediatrician what he thinks.

INFANT-STRENGTH SIMETHICONE DROPS. This relatively innocuous anti-gas medication (Mylicon is a popular brand) can sometimes help a gassy, miserable baby feel more comfortable. Of course, get your pediatrician's approval first.

SALINE NOSE DROPS. Use these sparingly to loosen up seriously gunky noses. Saline drops are also likely to deliver good booger-clearing sneezes and a pretty-ticked-off baby. Follow up with a nasal syringe if necessary. You'll find sterile saline drops in the baby care or cold-relief aisle. Tip: When you use saline drops, hold your baby upright and briskly spray the saline up into his nose. Don't lay him back and squeeze because you'll get a garden-hose torrent as opposed to a gentle spray. No one will be happy.

ANTIBIOTIC OINTMENT. An antibiotic ointment will be good to have on hand—especially with toddlers in the house. Applied to minor scrapes and cuts, it may help minimize the chance of infection and will probably help you feel better since you'll feel like you're doing something.

HYDROCORTISONE. You'll need this at some point to take down the redness and swelling that comes with rashes and insect bites. Any generic brand is fine; .05% is usually the recommended concentration for babies, but ask your pediatrician just to be sure.

ELECTROLYTE REHYDRATION SOLUTION. If your pediatrician recommends that you give this to a child who has been vomiting or diahrrea-ing, you'll be glad to have it right on hand. Girlfriend vomiting vets strongly recommend going for the CLEAR variety, as opposed to purple grape or red cherry flavors. If the stuff should come back up, clear will be far easier to get out of the carpet and the couch upholstery.

CALIBRATED MEDICINE DROPPER. Buying one of these is basically unnecessary, since most infant medications now come with built-in measuring droppers. If you are picking up a prescription, your pharmacist will generally include a medicine syringe or dropper in the bag. If he doesn't, ask him for one—preferably a syringe, since they tend to be more accurate and easier to use. It shouldn't cost you a penny.

SYRUP OF IPECAC. This induces vomiting in certain poisoning situations. Use only under the direction of a poison-control expert or your child's physician.

ACTIVATED CHARCOAL. This, too, is used in certain cases of poisoning.

FIRST-AID MANUAL. Ask your pediatrician to recommend one.

EMERGENCY CONTACT LIST. Contacts should include the phone number for Poison Control, the pediatrician, etc. Copies of the list should be taped inside the medicine cabinet, inside the first-aid kit(s), inside a kitchen cabinet, and other key spots around the house. For more on this, see Chapter 8.

What to Skip:

BATH RING OR BATH SEAT. These are designed to suction to the bottom of the tub and provide extra support for rookie sitters while they're taking a bath. Unfortunately, too many people have mistaken bath rings as a substitute for their own vigilance. As a result, inadequately tended babies have tipped over or slipped out of their bath ring and drowned. Many Girlfriends have truly loved their bath rings, even though they admit that the suction cups are piss poor; but since there is absolutely no margin for error here and the consequences can be fatal, we can't recommend them. There is no substitute for holding your not-quite-sitting-by-himself-yet baby with your own hands at all times while he's in the bath. That's probably what's best, anyway. If this means hopping into the tub with the little nipper, so be it.

BABY POWDER. Early on, using powder is a no-no, since breathing the stuff in can irritate a young baby's lungs. Down the road, a little baby cornstarch might be nice to sooth prickly-heat-puckered skin on the neck, under the arms, and behind the knees.

SUNBLOCK. Sunblock has generally not been tested on babies younger than six months of age. So the word is, you can't use it on babies who are younger than this. The best way to protect a young infant's skin is to limit or avoid exposure to direct or reflected sunlight. If this is totally impossible, use light clothing and a hat as protection.

OVER-THE-COUNTER COLD REMEDIES. Do not use any of these medications without first consulting your pediatrician.

CHAPTER NINE

Toys: Your Shortest Shopping List

There are three good reasons why you do not have to buy toys before your baby arrives. First, newborns can't hold up their own heads, much less hold up and actually play with any toys. Your face, your hands, and your voice will be their greatest source of delight. Second, you will most likely receive so many toys as gifts, you will not know where to put them. Third, you will add to the pile with your own impulse purchases once you are out and about with your babe and you discover how convenient it is to kill time in toy stores.

That said, we'll give you a rundown of Girlfriend insights on the infant-toy front:

- **Do Take Age Appropriateness Seriously.** We don't put much stock in all the developmental claims made by infant toy manufacturers. Frankly, babies are equally delighted (if not more so) by their mommy's car keys as they are by the colorful rattles that fill their toy basket. What we do like about toys that are specifically made for infants is that you can pretty much count on the fact that they are safe for him to play with. (There are no absolutes, as all those toy recalls can attest.) This means that the toys do not pose a choking hazard (a key point for children under three), are nontoxic, are free of points or sharp edges, and aren't so heavy that they'll bonk your baby and hurt his head.

- **Early On, Do Buy New.** Since young babies are under the distinct impression that toys belong first and foremost in their mouths, the Girlfriends just can't get comfortable with the idea of buying used rattles, teethers, and other mouth-bound infant toys. For that matter, we're sort of icked out by the thought of a babe inheriting them from anyone but an older sibling. The other big advantage of buying new is that the packaging gives you a good idea of what you're getting. It will tell you what age child the toy is intended for; it will tell you how the toy should be cleaned. Also important: If a toy is PVC or phthalate-free (which is the safest way to go with infant toys, since PVC may release toxins when it is sucked or chewed on for prolonged periods), the manufacturer will almost always make a point of saying so on the package. (Most of the big-name brands stopped using PVC in their infant teething toys since the issue hit the headlines in 1997; a good number have stopped using PVC period.)

- **Don't Overintellectualize.** Yes, young babies have fuzzy, limited eyesight at first. Yup, high-contrast colors and patterns may be easiest for them to see. It's not, in fact, a bad idea to have a few toys and objects that fit this description. But don't go nuts and fill the entire nursery with those expensive black, white, and red toys and accessories. First of all, the

Girlfriends pretty much agree that the stuff is butt ugly. Second, call it mother's intuition, but we think an overall nice, fuzzy view might be sort of soothing for a vulnerable creature who has just crawled out of a dark, wet womb. Third, the limited eyesight phenomenon is fleeting. Our doctor sources tell us infant eyesight drastically improves after about six months. That means when they're old enough to actually notice a toy or two, they won't need screaming patterns in black, white, and red to get their attention.

- **Don't forget who the toy is for.** The Girlfriends can't tell you how many colorful, quilted "activity" toys that we personally went gaga for have gone from toy basket to toy storage without getting even one whiff of attention from our babies. Even most of our teethers—with their adorable animal designs and irresistable chewy surfaces—went largely ungnawed. Early on, there simply is no way to tell what your baby is going to latch on to (other than your breasts). Babies, just like us grown-ups, don't all like the same things. A loud, bright busy box may delight one child, while it causes another to fall apart. Take it slowly and don't overinvest. Expose your baby to a variety of different objects (different textures, different sounds, etc.) and follow his cues. A couple of general points you might want to keep in mind, however:

- Toys should have features and gripping points that can be easily held by little hands and explored by tiny fingers.

- They should be lightweight.

- Teething babies seem to like gnawing on rather firm surfaces and objects—why else do cribs these days generally come with teething guards on the rails?

- If toys have a face—which babies do tend to like—it doesn't matter whose it is. So don't get sucked into the Disney marketing ploy du jour until your offspring force you to.

- Whatever you give to a child under age three should not present a choking hazard. A popular rule of thumb: If an object is too big to pass through a toilet paper tube, it's probably okay. Be careful, however, since some small stuffed toys and squeeze bath toys may look big enough but may actually fail this test when they are compressed.

- **Consider how you'll clean the stuff.** Look for toys that are easy to wipe down or surface wash. Even better: Opt for items that are machine washable or dishwasher safe.

- **Don't even think about buying stuffed animals . . . now.** We heard somewhere that if there was one thing parents thought their kids had too much of, it was stuffed animals. We easily believe this. The Girlfriends all have shelves, bins, baskets, and closets literally brimming with an entire animal kingdom's worth of stuffed toys that never get used. Mind you, we're not saying stuffed animals are bad or that babies don't enjoy them. We're saying that you will get more of these as gifts than your child will ever be able to play with. And chances are, the one he chooses as his transitional object will be some giveaway you got from the bank. Should you receive stuffed animals as gifts or if you find yourself unable to resist, give your young infant only the ones that have sewn eyes (as opposed to buttons or other doodads that can become detached and ingested) and are free of ribbons, strings, and other potential choke and strangulation hazards. Another word to the already wise:

Opt for plush, velvety-feeling critters as opposed to furry ones; you won't want your baby mouthing a stuffed animal and coming away with a kisser full of fuzz.

Play Equipment You May Want:

Before your baby can hold his head up, sit up, or stand up, most of your entertainment focus will be devoted to gear that holds him up or holds up itself. Here are some key pieces you might want to have:

Bouncy Seat: See details in Chapter 7
Stationary Exersaucer: Details, Chapter 7
Infant Activity Gym: Details, Chapter 7
Mobile: Details, Chapter 3

A Handful of Entertainment Options to Consider During Baby's First Year:

RATTLES. Opt for ones that are light and easy to grasp. Sassy makes some terrific, colorful rattles with lots of texture and those much-loved smiley faces on them.

INFANT MIRROR. Babies don't necessarily recognize themselves when they look in the mirror (come to think of it, you might feel the same way after a few months without sleep). They do, however, find their reflected face pretty entertaining. Lots of toy companies make soft, shatterproof mirrors that are safe to use with babies. Many infant mirrors are designed so they can tie onto the crib and lots of the Girlfriends have used them in this manner. If you do this, opt for a crib mirror that has very sturdy fasteners and a minimum of padding and puffiness.

BUSY BOX. Most of us Girlfriends had one of these in our own crib when we were babies. You know, there was a little dial that made a clicking noise, a button that squeaked when it was pushed, another gizmo that went "boing" when it was flicked. There are lots of updated models on the market—with all kinds of colorful lights, electronic music boxes, etc. If you decide you want one of these, choose a busy box that's not cushioned in any way (it's that SIDS thing again) and is free of sharp corners or projections that might catch on your baby's clothing. Fasten it to the side of the crib that's up against the wall so it can't be used as a foothold further down the road (same goes for the mirror or whatever else you attach to the crib rails). And keep it simple—anything that makes too much noise, lights up too much, or eats too many batteries will drive everyone crazy. Including, very possibly, your baby.

BOOKS. It's never too early to start—your babe may not seem enthralled, but you'll revel in this unparalleled motherhood moment. Sweet starters include:

- *Goodnight Moon* by Margaret Wise Brown, illustrated by Clement Hurd

- *The Runaway Bunny* by Margaret Wise Brown, illustrated by Clement Hurd

- *Big Red Barn* by Margaret Wise Brown, illustrated by Felicia Bond

- *Black on White* by Tana Hoban

- *The Carrot Seed* by Ruth Krauss, illustrated by Crockett Johnson

- *Jamberry* by Bruce Degen

- *Wheels on the Bus*

- *Good Night, Gorilla* by Peggy Rathmann

- *Jesse Bear, What Will You Wear?* by Nancy White Carlstrom, illustrated by Bruce Degen

- *Mr. Brown Can Moo, Can You?* Dr. Seuss

- *Guess How Much I Love You* by Sam McBratney, illustrated by Anita Jeram

- *The Very Busy Spider* by Eric Carle

- *The Going to Bed Book* by Sandra Boynton

- *The Snowy Day* by Ezra Jack Keats

Once your baby is past the blob stage, try these interactive attention getters:

- *Planes* by Byron Barton

- *Where's Spot?* by Eric Hill

- *Maisy's Big Flap Book* by Lucy Cousins

- *Pat the Bunny* by Dorothy Kunhardt

- *Fuzzy Yellow Ducklings* by Matthew Van Fleet

- *Open the Barn Door* by Christopher Santoro

- *Sweet Dreams, Sam* by Yves Got

- *The Mitten* by Jan Brett

- *Are You My Mother?* by P. D. Eastman

- *Chicka Chicka Boom Boom* by John Archambault and Bill Martin, Jr., illustrated by Lois Ehlert

- *Green Eggs and Ham* by Dr. Seuss

- *"Max"* books by Rosemary Wells

- *"Corduroy"* books by Don Freeman

- *My First Word Book (Revised Edition)* by Angela Wilkes

A BALL. Once your baby is sitting up, this is a key object to have on hand. Opt for something that's soft, light, fairly big, and eye-catching; if it has a little bell or other sound-making object inside, even better. Stay away from balls made from foam or any other material that can be easily bitten and ingested.

A SMALL POP-UP TENT OR HUT. A company named Play Hut makes a huge range of mini pop-up tents for tots. Buy one that's nice and small—rookie crawlers love to hide out and play in them.

PUSH TOY. It's a perfect choice for babies around their one-year birthday, since this is when many are starting or almost starting to walk. Fisher-Price makes some good basic activity walkers that are affordable and do the job just fine. Don't bother with the dolled-up versions with built-in electronic busy boxes. We've rarely seen a baby actually play with the busy box part of a push toy and it'll give you yet another reason to buy batteries.

Top Ten New Mommy Gifts

10. Cordless phone with headset. There is truly nothing more liberating than being able to hear which other Girlfriend thinks she's pregnant while nursing a baby, using the toilet, flushing, and Purelling.

9. Hemorrhoid doughnut pillow. Its not glamorous but she'll thank you later.

8. A nursing bra in black lace. I know they're as rare as hen's teeth, but they are such an affirmation of a future of lingerie that's as much for fun as for function.

7. Fruit of the Month Club, or some other such regular delivery of healthy food. Just when you're trying to convince yourself that sour-cream-and-onion potato chips represent the dairy and vegetable food requirements, a nice nectarine might come along.

6. Five hours a week of Merry Maids cleaning service or sharing your cleaning lady with the new mom. Leave the vacuuming to the mommy because it's an amazing way to put cranky newborns to sleep. If the cleaner only changes the towels and bed linens, it's bound to be a huge improvement.

5. Cool commuter cups, with spill-proof-lids. My first almost-walker pulled himself up on our coffee table and pulled my

mug of coffee down on his head. It's only by the grace of
God that I'd been awake and sipping from that mug for four
hours already and it was cold and coagulated. I've never left
a drink on a low surface again, even if my only companion is
my husband.

4. A pretty robe that wraps closed and readily absorbs liquids.
A good plush terry should be perfect. Remember, it must
have pockets big enough for TV remote, cordless phone, and
a four-ounce bottle, not to mention handfuls of tissue.

3. *The Girlfriends' Guide to Surviving the First Year of Motherhood.*
Suggest that Mom keeps it beside the toilet; she will be
spending a lot of time there trying to survive her first bowel
movement.

2. Digital camera and desktop 4×6 print developer. This is usually a gift from the grandparents because they are the grateful recipients of e-mail baby photos or spontaneous "brag
books" that the mom has put together without leaving the
house.

1. Jewelry. I've said it before and I'll say it again, jewelry of any
kind is a fabulous gift for a new mother. First of all, it com-
memorates the biggest event of her life, and second, it
almost always fits. Think charms, Tiffany heart bracelets
engraved with baby's name and birth date, pearl studs, or
the Hope Diamond.

CHAPTER TEN

The Padded Cell: Basic Babyproofing, Girlfriend Style

Sure, we can tell you to take care of this now. We can share stories about how we awakened one day to find our babies suddenly pulling up and ourselves completely hysterical. (Our Girlfriend Stacy became so convinced that her daughter was going to strangle herself on the Venetian blinds before she even got home from work, she called her baby-sister on the first day he pulled up and had the woman cut the cords off all her blinds with a pair of scissors.) We can tell you that having a baby will keep you busier than you ever imagined and that the idea of hunting down a gate and actually installing it will be so overwhelming, you'll put it off until the matter gets utterly urgent. We can tell you that your husband may end up banging on the door at Baby Depot at closing time, begging to be let in because his suddenly mobile baby's life is at risk. And chances are if he does come home with the goods, the gate won't fit or you will fight the entire time that you're both struggling to install it.

We're realists though, and we know that right now, you can barely imagine that that bump in your belly or bassinet will someday roll over, much less poke bobby pins into electrical outlets. You may nod your head agreeably about the importance of childproofing, but know that you're about as likely to tackle the entire task at this point as you are to begin researching local orthodontists. So, we'll take a moderate approach here and give you some basic food for thought.

FIRST, LOCATE A FEW SOURCES FOR GOOD, BASIC BABYPROOFING INFORMATION. The Consumer Product Safety Commission's Web site (*www.cpsc.gov*) is one dependable source; so is the National SAFE KIDS Campaign's *www.safekids.org*. There are also any number of books devoted to child and babyproofing. These include *Baby Proofing Basics* by Vicki Lansky and *Child Safe* by Mark A. Brandenburg, M.D. Your best bet is to keep one of these on hand as a troubleshooting reference.

SECOND, TAKE THIS WORD OF ADVICE FROM US: MAKING YOUR HOME A SAFE PLACE FOR YOUR BABY IS A LOT MORE ABOUT *DOING* THAN IT IS ABOUT *BUYING*. Indeed, there are a lot of gadgets out on the market, but from our own experience, these items are, themselves, often cheaply made and far from foolproof. Do all you can to childproof your home without too many special gadgets. Move detergents and other poisons up and completely out of reach. Get used to putting your pots on the back burner of the stove and turning the handles in. Lower the hot water heater to 120 F to help prevent burns from hot water (or install antiscald devices if you live in an apartment building). Get into the habit of closing the toilet lid— that is, of course, when you are not using it. Move furniture away from windows. If you live in a home or building that was built before 1978, get it tested for lead paint. (Call 800-424-LEAD for the name of a local lab that can do this for you; the EPA does not consider do-it-yourself home tests sufficient at this point.) Take an infant CPR and first-aid course during your third trimester (anything earlier and you'll forget what you've learned). Grow a second pair of eyes on the back of your head or look into a transplant. (We're only half kidding here.) And on and on and on. . . .

THIRD, SUSS OUT HOW EXTENSIVELY YOU'LL NEED TO CHILDPROOF. If you're in an older home with unusual moldings and fixtures, you might want to try out a couple of childproofing gadgets ahead of time to see if they'll even work for you. If you have a truly challenging situation—such as an open spiral staircase or a deck that poses a falling hazard—you might want to research professional child-proofers so you know who to call when you're ready to tackle the job. To locate the name of a childproofer in your area, check the Yellow Pages—try looking under "Baby Accessories," "Safety Consultants," or "Child Care Consultants." Or contact the International Association for Child Safety (888-677-IACS; *www.iafcs. org*). Keep in mind that this is not a certification agency but a referral service, so ask any candidate how many years of experience he has, make sure he has insurance that includes a term for "completed operations," which means the childproofer's work will still be covered after he has left the premises, and take the time to ring up his references.

FOURTH, DO THE ESSENTIALS NOW. Tackle the nursery. Install smoke and carbon monoxide detectors on every level of your home. If you have a dog, you will need to be able to separate the critter from your newborn without actually closing a door. If you live in a two-story home, a gate at the bottom of the stairs will keep the dog downstairs while your baby sleeps upstairs. Tie up Venetian blind cords; if you have blinds in the nursery, replace them with room-darkening shades. Check the aforementioned Web sites for other immediate "to dos."

When to Buy

As we said, take care of the essentials now. We'll give you four months to gain some footing after you deliver, then it's time to get cracking with the rest.

Where to Buy

You can get most of your childproofing gear right at the baby superstore. If you don't live near one or if you are searching for specialty childproofing items, check Kidco's Web site (*www.kidco-inc.com*). This company makes excellent safety gates and a wide array of other childproofing products. The site will give you an idea of what types of gadgets can address particular situations. Its "store finder" will also help you track down brick and mortar as well as Internet retailers who sell childproofing tools.

What You'll Probably Need

This list is by no means comprehensive; as we said, seek out detailed information from a book, safety Web site, or professional childproofer.

GATES. If you have stairs in your home, gates are a *must*. Mind you, we're not saying those gates necessarily have to go on the stairs. Several of the Girlfriends opted to install a gate on the nursery instead. This gave them a safe place to plop their little wanderer if Mom or Dad had to get some vacuuming done or run downstairs for something. A gate on the nursery also comes in handy when you liberate your babe from a crib to a big kid bed, since it keeps him safely in bounds but still within your ear- and eyeshot. Many of us who put gates on our stairs did very well installing them only at the top, as opposed to at both ends. (It may be erroneous thinking, but it seemed like a fall from the top of the stairs offered no margin for error, while one does have a greater opportunity to catch a crawler in the act when he's on his way up. Besides, once our babies were able to get themselves up the stairs they were less likely to tumble down them.) Should you decide to put gates at the top of your stairs, you must use a special type of gate intended for this purpose. TOP OF THE STAIRS GATES MUST ACTUALLY BE MOUNTED TO THE WALL OR MOLDING. IN SOME CASES, THEY CAN BE DIFFICULT TO INSTALL. IF YOU ARE HAVING PROBLEMS, YOU MAY WANT TO EAT THE COST AND CALL A CHILDPROOFER. Several Girlfriends (or their husbands) have had good luck installing and using gates from Kidco. If you decide to put gates at the bottom of the stairs, you could technically use a pressure gate (you kind of wedge these into place, as opposed to mounting them with hardware). But we have found them to be a hassle, since they always seemed to be falling out of position. You'll probably be better off—as some of us eventually were—installing "top of the stairs" style gates at the base of the stairs instead. In general, you should choose gates that have vertical slats, as opposed to a lattice or crisscross design that could provide a foothold for little climbers.

OUTLET PLUGS OR COVERS. Those little plastic plugs that go into unused outlets might fit tightly in your outlets, they might not. If they are easy to remove (meaning you don't need a key or a coin to pry them out and end up breaking at least one nail in the process), you'll probably need to replace your outlet covers with the child-safe variety that automatically obscures the outlet when it is not in use. Before you start working with gadgets, however, first see how many outlets can be covered by simply moving big pieces of furniture in front of them.

CABINET LATCHES. Go easy on these or you will go nuts. Do your best to consolidate poisons and dangerous items. Move whatever you can up and out of reach. The one cabinet all of the Girlfriends secured was the one under the kitchen sink. Even though we moved all big-time poisons out from there—such as Drano, etc.—we still found it unrealistic to keep dish soap, sponges, dishwasher detergent, the trash, and other basics anywhere else. Practically every parent on the planet leaves their Tupperware and plastic container cabinet unlocked since it provides some excellent entertainment for tykes and a good distraction from the off-limits stuff. Just get used to rinsing those containers before you use 'em.

DRAWER LATCHES. These somewhat annoying little gadgets prevent young children from being able to open a drawer more than only a few inches. By pushing down on a little plastic catch, Mom and Dad have a slightly better shot at it. You'll probably need latches on any drawer in your kitchen that holds sharp or small objects; you might also need latches on the drawers in your bathrooms.

FURNITURE ANCHORS. These will prevent bookshelves, dressers, and other furniture from tipping over on your child. Look for Mommy's Helper Tip-Resistant Furniture Safety Brackets.

COFFEE TABLE BUMPER OR CORNER GUARDS. Coffee tables are the perfect height for incurring some serious head bonks to crawling babies and rookie walkers. To combat this problem, some of us Girlfriends have used something called a table bumper, a sort of big puffy snood that wraps around the entire perimeter of the table. It's pretty hideous looking, but the bumper can be popped off in a jiff when grown-up company comes over. Unfortunately, the very fact that these bumpers can be removed so easily is what made them useless for Girlfriends with particularly dexterous toddlers. Among this contingent, some of us bought childproofing "corner guards" and wedged them onto the corners of the table. This helped somewhat, but the guards did nothing to prevent our babies from hitting their heads on the unshielded sides of the table. For many of us, the best solution was to move the coffee table out of the middle of the room until our babies were steady on their feet. Sounds harsh, but look at it this way: You won't be doing much in the way of fancy entertaining over the next many months, and you'll be freeing up some nice play space for your baby and his buddies.

FIREPLACE BUMPER. If you have a fireplace and it's in a room you use a lot, you may want to wrap the hearth in one of these to soften the edges. Check the babyproofing catalogs and Web sites for options.

Part 2

Gearing up the Rest of Your Life

CHAPTER ELEVEN

Hunkering Down for the Hurricane— from Cleaning Carpets to Stocking the Kitchen

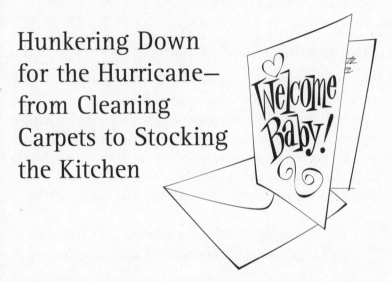

Here we are, Girlfriend to Girlfriend. We've shared all we have to share about what that beautiful little baby of yours will need. Now, let's talk about what you can do and buy to make your own adjustment easier.

Prep the House

Once your baby arrives, you will have more to do than ever before. Yet you will have less time, fewer hands, and far less mobility to tackle it all. To top it off, your brain will be so addled from the combined effects of sleep deprivation and baby bliss, you won't even be able to entertain the idea of how it should all get done. We beg you to lay the groundwork now that will help you handle the onslaught to come. Having a sense of control over some part of your environment will help you surrender to and even revel in the utter chaos that your unpredictable, magnificently defiant little baby will bring.

Clear Up Existing Clutter, Prepare for More

Most real baby prep gets jammed into the last few months of pregnancy because it simply seems presumptuous to get carried away too early on. Yet earlier on, most of us are bristling to at least do something. Take this opportunity to clear the decks of your current life. Put everything that's *not* in order *in* order, because believe us, if you don't do it before the baby arrives, you'll have to wait till your last one leaves for college to catch up. Our top suggestions:

- Put all existing, free-floating photos in albums or photo boxes; buy several extra photo boxes to accommodate what's soon to come.

- Organize your closets.

- If you don't already have an existing file for household bills, documents, etc., create one (see below) and put all those papers in order.

- Give away or sell stuff you don't want.

- Create advance storage space. This could be your attic, a corner of a room, or your parent's basement. Buy two or more big plastic storage bins (or save some big cardboard boxes), keep them empty, and put them in your "storage" spot. When your baby starts growing out of her clothes and toys (which will happen very quickly), you'll know exactly where these things should go. Hold on to empty wet-wipe containers along the way—they are great for storing teethers, rattles, and other small items.

- Organize often-used paraphernalia by category into separate, portable, and labeled "work" boxes. Keep these boxes on an easily accessible shelf in a high-traffic room or disperse them in strategic spots throughout the house. This will encourage you to tackles tasks whenever the opportunity arises and wherever you may be. You can buy plastic bins for this job (try Staples; the Container Store, *www.containerstore.com*, or your warehouse club); shoe boxes do just fine, too. Candidates include:

CORRESPONDENCE BOX. Do this for sure so you can keep up with all those thank-you notes and bills. Fill it with the essentials—your address book, a small notebook for logging who gave what and who's been thanked, thank-you cards (they can match your announcements or not), pens, BIG rolls of stamps, some blank legal-size envelopes, and preprinted return-address labels (you've probably gotten plenty as "gifts" from all of those charity solicitations).

FIX-IT BOX. Put together a small toolbox with all the everyday essentials like duct tape, glue, Phillips and flathead screwdrivers, and a variety of batteries (you will use these often to assemble and "rejuice" baby equipment).

GIFT-WRAP BOX. Think tape, scissors, ribbon, cards (you won't believe how many birthday parties you will be attending); keep a stash of gift wrap in a closet somewhere. A small cache of generic gifts might be wise, too.

EMERGENCY SEWING BOX. If you don't already have a sewing box, a mini version with a few needles, buttons, and spools of thread should do it. (Not a few of us have foregone wearing a pair of pants for a full year because we couldn't get around to sewing a button back on.)

CAMERA SUPPLY BOX. Include ample film, batteries, cleaning supplies, operating manuals, a Sharpie pen to identify videotapes.

Create a Central Family File

You won't believe the amount of paperwork a pregnancy and the ensuing baby will generate. There are hospital records, medical records, birth certificates, product warranties and instruction manuals (not for the baby, unfortunately), all of which will need to go somewhere. You'll be collecting info about mommy and me classes, lactation consultants, and baby-sitters. Don't wait until you're facing an intimidating six-foot-high pile of documents to create a home for this stuff. Set yourself up now so all you need is to open a drawer to get papers out of your sight and into the right place.

Top Suggestions:

1. Buy a three-drawer file cabinet (you'll fill it eventually) and keep it somewhere that's easily accessible for you but out of the baby's way (those corners can be sharp). A corner or a closet in your own bedroom are good options.

2. Stock up on filing supplies. Half the reason why stuff never gets filed is because it doesn't have anywhere to go. Having the right materials on hand will make a big difference. Buy several boxes of hanging files, manila folders, labels, and whatever else you think you might need. If

you need to make this exciting, buy fancy colors. For the office-supply-addicted among us, a trip to Staples is heaven.

3. Create files for what you've collected so far; fill the file drawer with lots of unused hanging files and put unmarked tabs on them. When rogue papers enter the house, all you'll need to do is pick up one of those babies, fill in the label ("baby gear instruction manuals" or "baby-friendly vacation ideas" or "spas I want to go to when baby graduates from college"), and file it away. Must-have files you might want to set up in advance (this is by no means all-inclusive):

- Insurance Information (background information; forms; pending claims; paid claims)

- Hospital Records (Registration paperwork; bills; birth paperwork, birth certificate—if you don't keep it in a separate vital records file)

- Birth Mementos (hospital bracelet, hospital cap, "It's a Boy!" card from the isolette)

- Baby's Medical Records (individual physician info; bills; baby medical record notebook (see sidebar); folders for specific medical issues, eg., Acid Reflux, January 2004; Chipped Tooth, May 2004; Broken Pinkie, April 2005)

- Vital Papers (birth certificate; Social Security cards; etc.)

- Financial Records (savings bonds; trusts, etc.)

- Baby Registry and Baby Gifts (registry list, list of who gave what)

- Baby Gear Information (notes; instruction manuals; warranties)

- Classes and Activities (Info on baby-care classes, mommy and me classes)

- Baby-sitter/Day-care Information

- And so on, and so on, and so on . . .

Keep a Baby Health Record Notebook

Our Girlfriend Caitlin keeps a small spiral notebook for each of her children. She brings the notebook with her to the pediatrician each time she visits. In it she jots down questions she has for the doctor so she won't forget to ask them. She also records the reason for the visit (checkup, ear infection, etc.) Besides being functional, these little books have been wonderful mementos for Caitlin and her girls. Caitlin, in fact, has the book her mother kept for her and can't believe she ever weighed 47 pounds.

Get On-line

If you aren't on the Internet already, seriously consider doing it now. Cyberspace is not only a great place to shop for baby supplies and research childrearing issues, it will also provide you with a much-welcome lifeline during what can be a very isolating and immobile time. Bookmark key sites—see our Top 10 list on this subject.

Do Basic Babyproofing and Safety Musts:

See Chapter 10 for details.

Tackle Those Baby Announcements

Oh, how the Girlfriends would like to believe that the day of cyber-announcements has finally arrived. It really would make life a whole lot easier and save a forest worth of trees. But with lots of pre-Internet relatives and friends still around, we just don't think cyber announcements cut the mustard quite yet. As far as snail-mail announcements go, we recommend, like every baby book in the universe, that you order them during your seventh month and address the envelopes in advance. Then all you'll need to do is call with the vitals after your baby arrives. A last thought: Girlfriends who have given birth during the last three months of the year have generally chosen to combine their baby announcements with their holiday cards. If you're not big on formalities, you might want to consider this option. Vicki did this three times, using insert cards for her announcements.

Join Your Local Warehouse Club

Saving money isn't the only advantage of joining a warehouse store. Those bulk packages can seriously help you cut down on shopping trips—a major plus when you're relatively housebound with a young baby (as long as you have room to store the stuff). To avoid fraying your own nerves as well as your baby's, make warehouse shopping a chore for your partner if possible. (Or at least go while someone else is watching the baby.) To escape what our Girlfriend Cindy's husband calls pickled-egg syndrome, create a set list of warehouse staples and stick to it so you don't end up with oddities that seemed like a bargain but really just jacked up your bill. Key household items worth stocking up on: paper goods, soaps and detergents, film, batteries (you'll need lots of these—baby gear tends to use sizes C, A, and AA), plastic garbage and storage bags, diapers, wipes, formula, and jarred baby food. Other good buys: wrapping paper (often sold in handy kits complete with coordinating ribbon and gift cards); and food staples that can last on the shelf or in the freezer, like pasta, chicken breasts, and dried cereal.

Stock the Kitchen

Your Girlfriends may very well import some good eats once baby arrives, but you should still stock the place like you're expecting a major hurricane. Some key items you might want to have:

PAPER PLATES AND PLASTIC UTENSILS: You can worry about the environment a little later. These may save your sanity on particularly hairy days.

SPILLPROOF-COMMUTER MUGS: Retire your current coffee mugs and cups for the forseeable future and replace them with a bunch of lidded, insulated cups that commuters use. They're harder to spill, easy to schlepp around (don't do it with your baby in your arms if the drink is hot), and have a shot at keeping your drink semi cold or hot while you get sidetracked cleaning spit-up from the rug.

WATER BOTTLES: Save the bottles with the pull-up squirt tops that sports drinks and commercial water often come in. They'll come in very handy while you're nursing, since you'll be drinking all the time in all kinds of places.

SHELF-STABLE MILK: Buy the juice-box size containers. It tastes a tad different from fresh milk, but you will thank heaven for it on those mornings you absolutely must have your cup of decaf and there ain't a single fresh dairy product in the fridge. Shelf-stable milk will continue to save the day when your baby is old enough to drink cow's milk in his bottle and you still aren't together enough to have fresh dairy in the fridge at all times. Shelf-stable milk boxes are also great for traveling and camping.

READY-MADE MEALS: If some good Girlfriend or auntie doesn't whip up soups or casseroles for you, go ahead and buy some frozen and canned stuff—lasagna, Lean Cuisines, etc. This may seem like a sorry alternative right now, but you will be grateful to have it on hand. Even if it's for your husband.

FLOUR TORTILLAS: If these aren't already a family staple, consider entering them on the roster. Flour tortillas stay fresh in the fridge for eons so they're easy to keep on hand. Wrap them around some scrambled eggs, some odd scraps of takeout chicken, or just melt some cheddar cheese inside, and you can turn a pretty sorry dinner situation into a somewhat solid meal.

CANNED OR FROZEN SOUPS

FROZEN AND DRIED PASTAS

PREPARED PIZZA CRUSTS (LIKE BOBOLI): Throw anything on it—except ice cream—and it's a meal.

PARMESAN CHEESE: It keeps forever and can turn just about any old thing into something edible.

CANNED TUNA: Right out of the can, with a squirt of lemon, it's a better bet than junk food.

PEANUT BUTTER AND JELLY: Get reintroduced. It will be saving your butt for a long time to come.

BREAD: Always keep a loaf in the freezer.

LOVELY DECAF COFFEES AND TEAS: They don't spoil and they'll be a welcome treat when you're sitting awake in your robe at 3:30 P.M. or 3:30 A.M.

A FILE FULL OF DELIVERY AND TAKE-OUT MENUS: Start collecting these as soon as you find out you're pregnant.

Clean the Carpets

You have no idea of how much time you will be spending on the floor over the next couple of years. Start your baby out on something that's not too grubby. Schedule a deep, steam clean during your last month of pregnancy.

Post Emergency Lists

Type up a list on your computer—it should include 911; the number for Poison Control; your family's full name, your address and cross streets; your and your partner's work and cell phone numbers; your pediatrician's address and phone number; your pharmacy; and personal emergency contacts (at least a couple of them should be very local). After the baby is born you should add his full name, his birth date, and any existing health conditions. Post a large version of this list in the kitchen. Some of us have also printed out the list in a smaller format and taped it to the back of the phones in the house.

Deal with Some of the Really Grown-up Stuff

We're talking specifically about wills and life insurance. Even if you don't nail down all the details now (which wouldn't be the worst idea), determine who you want to work with and what you want to do. Then, when you bolt upright in bed one night, realizing your child is already two and has no legal guardian, all it will take is a quick call to get the wheels in motion.

Invest in Key Mom-Friendly Accoutrements

You won't find these in any baby gear or maternity store. But let us tell you, they are among the handiest things a new mom can have:

CLEAR PLASTIC SHOWER CURTAIN: Ah, the joy of showering while you're alone in the house with a young baby. You're nervous because you can't see your precious angel. He's hysterical because Mommy's suddenly disappeared. Here's how you can both keep an eye on each other: Put up a clear plastic shower curtain, and place your baby in his bouncy seat on the bathroom floor while you bathe. It's no guarantee against tears, but you'll probably be able to get all your conditioner out. (If you don't want the whole world to see your cellulite, keep an opaque curtain up along with the clear and pull it back when you are alone with the baby.)

CORDLESS PHONE WITH A HEADSET: The phone isn't just a tool for tracking down the plumber and cursing out cold callers. It can be a very important lifeline and isolation breaker for a new, relatively housebound mom. A phone equipped with a headset will increase your chances of actually having a decent conversation because you won't need your already overcommitted hands to hold it. It will also spare you from going into traction because you won't be holding the receiver in the crook of your neck for weeks on end. Early on, when you're not even close to wearing anything the receiver can clip on to, stick it in the pocket of your bathrobe. Down the road, hang it on your waistband.

DUSTBUSTERS: Crumbs of every imaginable kind will soon invade every corner of your life. We're not just talking about your baby's mess, but your own, since you will rarely have the chance to actually eat a meal at a table. Cheerios, rice grains, crushed Zwieback, and smushed Goldfish crackers will mingle with traces of Mommy's and Daddy's potato chips, rice cakes, and God knows what else on the the kitchen floor. The food bits will crawl behind the couch cushions, infiltrate your sheets, and overtake your car. Have portable vacuums on hand, Girlfriend, because you will never in a million years keep up if you have to haul a big machine out of the closet. Certainly, put one portable vac in the kitchen, and if possible, one on every floor of the house. An electric broom or lightweight stick vacuum is also pretty handy.

PUMP-TOP SOAPS AND HAND LOTION AT EVERY SINK: You'll constantly be changing diapers; interlopers from the outside world will want to touch that precious baby. Pump-top soaps (antibacterial in the beginning if the idea excites you) make it easy for everyone to get their grubby grown-up hands clean; hand lotion will help keep your own mitts from morphing into leather.

MAGAZINE SUBSCRIPTIONS: You probably won't have the opportunity to plow through any great Russian fiction after your baby epic begins, but magazines—some good gossipy ones, some that focus on parenting—will provide welcome company while you're nursing for the nineteenth hour straight and everyone else is asleep or at the mall. Subscribe to a bunch a couple of months before you're due—think *Child*, *InStyle*, and *Allure*. Later on you'll be thrilled to get something in the mail that doesn't have "please remit" on the envelope.

CHAPTER TWELVE

Prepping Yourself

Mom's To-Do Time Line

OK, Girlfriends, now let's talk about what you should do for you.

First Trimester

GET A CELL PHONE AND A DATE BOOK/HANDHELD ORGANIZER. If you don't already have these appendages, pick 'em up now. From this point on, you'll want to have easy access to all the important players in your pregnant life (namely, your partner, your OB, and your best Girlfriends). You'll also have to start keeping track of all those doctor's appointments—for yourself, and for your babe, once he arrives.

Second Trimester

SEE THE DENTIST. Getting to the dentist might be a laughable concept after the baby arrives. Besides, good oral health is crucial while you are pregnant, since certain oral complications have been linked to preterm delivery. Schedule an appointment during your second trimester, since you may be too big later to sit comfortably in that dentist chair.

Third Trimester

GET YOUR HAIR CUT. Get a nice, cleaned-up cut during your last month. It will perk up your spirits and give you an extra opportunity to take a load off those swollen feet. Don't go too short, however, or you'll regret how it makes you look like a bloated Q-tip. You'll then be contending with the desire to grow out a new do when you have a few other things to think about.

PACK YOUR BAG FOR THE HOSPITAL. We talk at length in the *Girlfriends' Guide to Pregnancy* about what to bring to the hospital when the big day finally arrives. Here's a brief recap:

A soft, comfy going-home outfit for yourself (you will still be
   fat). A maternity outfit is not out of the question.

Flat shoes to wear home

Your makeup bag

A robe

A nursing bra

Maternity underwear

2–3 pairs of thick, cotton socks

Soft, flat bedroom slippers

Your own shampoos, soaps, and lotions

Lip balm

Hair dryer
Hairbrush
Hair scrunchies or clips
Toothbrush and toothpaste
Eyeglasses
Pen
A book on breastfeeding
Cameras and film
Your telephone list
Insurance card
Hospital preregistration papers
Calling card

FOR BABY:
Baby's car seat (Dad or another person can actually bring it
    when they come to visit)
Side snap T-shirt
Going-home outfit
A receiving blanket

Don't Bother:

A NIGHTGOWN: The fluids gushing out of you will only ruin it. Use your robe when you want to walk around without your hiney popping out of your hospital gown.

NURSING PADS: The hospital will provide them if needed.

JEWELRY: It will only get stolen. If you haven't already taken off your rings (due to sausage-sized fingers) remove these, too.

Put Together Your Postpartum Recovery Kit:

Regardless of the fact that hospitals like to boot new moms out before we even memorize our room number, we're still essentially hospital patients when we come home. We are still leaking from many different spots, our stitches aren't healed, our various systems are somewhat off kilter. The bottom line: Our body desperately needs a chance to recover. Here are some basic items that you should have awaiting you back home:

2 NICE-LOOKING SETS OF (NURSING-FRIENDLY, IF APPLICABLE) PAJAMAS AND A PRETTY ROBE: Remind yourself and everybody else of your "recovering patient status" by staying in your pajamas as much as possible for at least one week—and ideally two—after you get home. (Do it with your first baby, it will be near impossible the next time around.) You'll be more inclined to stick by your guns if you have jammies that don't make you look like Oscar Madison. You can buy actual nursing pajamas if you intend to breast-feed. But try those babies on while you're still in the store and actually attempt popping your breast out of those handy built-in breast slits. Many of us who didn't try before buying had to resort to literal breast gymnastics due to the fact that the nursing slits were too small for our humongous, milk-engorged mammaries or were positioned in the perfect place if only our breasts had been located somewhere up near our clavicle. Frankly, most of us were happiest wearing normal two-piece pajamas and simply lifting the top slightly when our babies needed to feed. Nightgowns with buttons down the front work, too. One last thought: Even if you give birth in the depths of winter, pass up heavy flannel or fleece for 100 percent lightweight cotton. As we mention below, postpartum women can sweat buckets. Add a small human perpetually clutched to your torso, and you can pretty much guess how toasty things can get. If you do get chilly at some point, you can throw on your robe. Choose one that's soft, provides easy breast access, has big pockets, and ISN'T PLAID!

TUCKS: You may get some of these witch-hazel-soaked pads from the hospital. Buy some just in case—they'll be very soothing to your pudendum, whether you wind up with an episiotomy or not.

NURSING PADS: One box will do for starters. For details, see Chapter 6.

BIG SPANKY UNDERPANTS: Things stay pretty leaky and messy for at least a few weeks after you deliver. You'll need big undies with room to accommodate those gigantic maxi-pads and you won't want to have to think twice about pitching them once they get stained with God knows what's emanating from you. Buy a bunch of big, cheap cotton beauties from somewhere glamorous, like Wal-Mart.

SANITARY NAPKINS: Get the biggest, maxiest ones available. If you're tremendously self-assured (or are gushing so heavily you suspect that only a roll of Bounty will do the job), you might want to do what our Girlfriend Gwen did her second time around: Toss in your dignity chips, buy some adult diapers, and wear those until the flow slows. Just don't look in the mirror.

NIPPLE BALM: You may need medical-grade lanolin or Aquaphor for your inevitably sore nipples, if you plan to nurse. For details, see Chapter 6.

WATERPROOF MATTRESS COVER: In case nobody else bothers to tell you, it's not uncommon at all for postpartum women to sweat their water weight out in their sleep. We're not talking about a nice sheen. We're not talking about merely perspiring. We're talking about waking up in sheets that are so soaked, you're convinced that a pipe burst in your ceiling overnight. Spare your mattress the abuse and keep a waterproof cover on it. If you put it on during your third trimester, you'll also be protected should your water break while you're in bed.

Other Important To-Do's for You: Plan for the Great Cover-up

When the Girlfriends were freshly minted mothers, the mere thought of putting something other than pajamas onto our alien bodies was enough to make us hole up in the house like Howard Hughes. We didn't have a prayer of fitting into our prepregnancy duds. We were so damned sick of our maternity clothes, we just couldn't bear the idea of putting them back on. The cruel irony was that at that vulnerable, "I have nothing to put on my body" moment of life, people were snapping pictures of the baby (who was inevitably in our arms) every two seconds. To this day, those photos are on display at every Grandma's house and in key family photo albums. Yours will be, too.

What's a Girlfriend to do? If you've got cash to burn, you could go out and buy a temporary wardrobe in a larger size. For most of us though, spending what clothing budget we had on a load of stuff that we would hopefully get limited mileage out of was unthinkable. If we were going to go on a shopping spree, it wasn't gonna be for temporary tents and muumuus.

We don't have a foolproof solution to this pickle (other than disappearing to a nudist retreat for several months). Just some tips that may tide you over:

1. **Think Way Ahead.** Your postpartum body will be very similar to the body you have during your first trimester, only fatter. It'll be puffy and thick, but without that obvious bulge that makes you a candidate for traditional maternity clothes. If you are still in the early part of your pregnancy and intend to buy bigger transitional clothes before you start wearing maternity stuff, buy three season items so you have a shot at being able to wear them after the baby arrives. For example, stay away from heavy wool and suffocating synthetics. Buy short sleeves—you can always wear a cardigan over them. If you intend to nurse, keep that in mind, too: Choose shirts that button down or can lift up easily; pass up dresses, unless they have buttons down the front of the bodice. Better yet, opt instead for a flowing skirt with an elastic waist and put a loose shirt on top. When you do start shopping for real maternity clothes, consider European-style garments that have a wide stretchy waistband that sort of "grows" with your belly, as opposed to the traditional belly "pouch." This type of maternity design is becoming ever more popular. It will also be more appealing and easier for you to wear postpartum.

2. **Borrow . . . from the right people.** You can't very well ask a chunky Girlfriend if you can use some of her regular clothes as your "fat" clothes. But if your mom is bigger than you are, you can probably ask her without putting her nose too far out of joint. Even a couple of blouses that can accommodate your bigger-than-ever breasts can be a big help. If you will be borrowing maternity clothes from Girlfriends, don't forget to ask them if they have any postpartum "transitional" clothes they (hopefully) no longer need. Of course, also go right back into your husband's

wardrobe and use whatever you can. His button-downs will be indispensible—as nursing shirts and as butt covers.

3. **Buy a few key pieces.** Think specifically about what's coming up in the first couple of months postpartum. If you're like most Girlfriends, you're not going to have a million occasions which each call for a different kind of outfit. More than likely, your postpartum wardrobe needs will break down something like:

ONE SPECIAL OCCASION OUTFIT (the bris, the baptism, or some relative or friend's birthday or anniversary you just can't miss): You'll be in great shape if you have a long black skirt with a stretchy waistband from your maternity wardrobe. If you don't, buy a long black skirt postpartum and cover your derriere with an oversize cardigan, unconstructed jacket, or blouse.

TOTALLY COMFORTABLE, QUASI-JAMMIES: Do your best not to spend all your time in sweats. As Seinfeld once said to George, and we're paraphrasing here, it really does look like you've given up. Look for soft cotton-knit lounge pants and shorts—lots of the catalogs, like Garnet Hill, J. Jill, and Victoria's Secret, sell them. Fitness catalogs and athletic stores sell "yoga" pants that can do the trick, too. Top these off with any oversize T-shirt you have. When you start wearing normal clothes again, you'll still be happy to have comfy garb like this to wear around the house and even sleep in.

THE DASHING-OUT OUTFIT: Buy one or two pairs of elastic-waisted, unconstructed pants and wear them to death. If you stick with benign colors like black or tan, it will be harder for people to notice that you've been wearing the same thing every day for two months. If it's summer, pick up some shorts that pretty much fit this description; bike shorts (with a big shirt, of course) are another handy thing to have. A couple of loose (but not sloppy) T-shirts or long-sleeved polos will look cute and will serve you well if you're nursing. Avoid solid black or white on top since these colors tend to show off milk, formula, and spit-up stains particularly well.

CLOGS, SLIDES, SLIP-ONS: Simplify your life and forget about shoelaces. Find shoes that slip on as easily as they slip off. You will appreciate having them when you have to spring up from snuggling with your angel on the playroom floor, so you can run out the front door and catch the UPS man or sprint to the A&P for formula at ten o'clock at night. Vicki loves clogs; they're sturdy and easy to slip on, but still add height.

Mobilize the Troops

As we have said so many times before, now is not the time to prove to the world how independent you can be. It is not the time to tough it out, suck it up, or hold it all in.

We've spent this entire book describing all of the "things" that will help you take care of your baby and ease your transition to motherhood. The irony is, they don't compare to what other human beings can offer. We can't urge you enough to not only accept help, but to go out and ask for it. It may cost you money, it may cost you some pride, but believe us, it will pay off in the end. Because you will be a stronger and more capable mother for it. Trust us, you give people gifts when you accept their help.

FIND A SUPPORTIVE PEDIATRICIAN. Start interviewing candidates during your second trimester. The doctor you choose should take an interest in your welfare—your breast-feeding progress, your emotional state—as well as your baby's. Check *The Girlfriends' Guide to Pregnancy* for particulars.

CONSIDER HIRING A BIRTH DOULA. These nonmedical birth assistants are trained to provide support and encouragement for women before and during childbirth. If you and/or your partner are a bit apprehensive about the labor and delivery process or if you simply feel you might appreciate having an extra advocate with you during childbirth, this might be worth looking into. Contact Doulas of North America (888-788-DONA; *www.dona.org*) for further information and names of practitioners in your area.

LOCATE A LACTATION CONSULTANT. If you intend to nurse, seek out a lactation consultant during your second trimester, and put her on your speed dial. See more on these breast-feeding gurus in Chapter 6.

SCOUT OUT AND JOIN A SUPPORT GROUP. Those new-mommy groups offered by community organizations and hospitals provide relief from the social isolation that comes with having a new baby. For many Girlfriends, our group meeting was the only actual event we got dressed for each week, and it was where many of our friendships began. The "baby blues" and postpartum depression are real, and while they don't affect all new moms, no one should *ever* think twice about reaching out.

LINE UP HELP AT HOME. Consider support at home as crucial to your recovery as any medical care, especially during the first two weeks. If a postpartum doula or nurse is simply not economically feasible, ask friends or family members (as long as they won't drive you up a wall).

FIND A DOG WALKER, IF APPLICABLE, AND PAY FOR THE SERVICE IF YOU HAVE TO. We're not just talking about while you're in the hospital, but for at least the first few weeks after you and the baby come home and everyone else has returned to work or their own lives. Even some help once a day will make a difference.

HIRE SOMEONE TO CLEAN THE HOUSE. Shortly before you're due (or even while you're in the hospital), get a cleaning service to do a thorough top-to-bottom scrub down of the place. It will feel great to bring your nice, clean babe into a nice, clean abode. Then again, you may be hormonally driven to do it yourself.

LINE UP SOME KIND OF BABY-SITTING HELP. Two or three hours a couple of times a week can give you just enough time to regroup. Find a high school or local college student—even if you're not comfortable leaving her alone in the house with the baby, you'll appreciate the extra set of arms and the company. Late afternoons are usually ideal, since new moms and new babes tend to unravel around that time and dinner prep is looming. It ain't called "The Witching Hour" for nothin'.

PUT YOUR PARTNER TO WORK. If he has no clue about what he's supposed to do, go ahead and tell him. And don't get all caught up in how he does it—as long as what he's doing isn't dangerous (like when our Girlfriend Elizabeth's husband gave the baby a plastic grocery bag to play with). When he gets home from work, don't feel bad about handing over the baby. Don't think twice about having him change the diapers or do the wash. And don't stick yourself with night duty all the time based on the premise that

Daddy has to get up for work tomorrow. You'll have work tomorrow, too, and if you get sick, everyone's job and life will be affected.

TURN TO YOUR GIRLFRIENDS. We are the ones who will hold you while you cry and hold that sweet, precious baby while you sleep. We are the ones who will take you on that first stroll out in the world and reassure you every step of the way. We'll show you the best nursing spots in town and stare down any nosybody who takes an interest. We will give you the clothes off our backs and the food out of our fridges. We will do anything we can to help you and your baby because we have been there. The friendship of another Mom doesn't have an expiration date. It won't go out of style. And it doesn't cost a penny. It is, quite simply, the best investment an expectant mom like you can make. Now, get out of here and go shopping!

10 WEB SITES TO BOOKMARK

American Academy of Pediatrics, www.aap.org: Extensive info and news on child health and safety, including child sleepwear guidelines and a listing of all new car seats sold in the U.S. with all their specs.

National SAFEKIDS Campaign, www.safekids.org: Wide-ranging site focusing on child safety.

Epinions, www.epinions.com: See what other parents are saying about the baby products you're considering on this huge consumer opinion site.

U.S. Consumer Product Safety Commission, www.cpsc.gov: Source for product safety information; subscribe to their recall alert list, and they'll e-mail you if something is announced.

National Highway Traffic Safety Administration, www.nhtsa.dot.gov: Accurate source for car-seat information, as well as general child passenger safety advice.

La Leche League International, www.lalecheleague.org: Definitive, albeit opinionated, source for breastfeeding info.

Babystyle, www.babystyle.com: Even if you don't buy anything, this site will give you an idea of what's in style and what type of specialty items are hot.

Babycenter, www.babycenter.com: Good, general articles for new and expectant parents; e-mails personalized to your baby's age, and a solid store with helpful consumer reviews.

Babies 'Я' Us, www.babiesrus.com: Good for shopping as well as research.

Ebay, www.ebay.com: Don't assume this auction site is a place for secondhand stuff and offbeat collectibles. Retailers and surplus houses unload overstocks of brand spankin' new baby products at amazing prices here. This includes names like Peg Perego and other specialty brands that are traditionally unavailable at discount.

THINGS TO DO FOR YOURSELF BEFORE BABY ARRIVES (BECAUSE WHO KNOWS WHEN YOU'LL HAVE ANOTHER CHANCE?)

Organize existing photos

Get haircut

See dentist

Eat out at places that are not child friendly

See movies

Drive with your favorite CDs cranked

Hang out at department store cosmetic counters; have in-depth chats with makeup ladies

Get a manicure (bring your own manicure set)

Read

Sleep late

TOP ITEMS TO BORROW/INHERIT

Stationary Exerciser

Baby bathtub

Baby Björn

Bouncy seat

Infant Side-snap T-shirts

Unused disposable nursing pads

Prams

Carriage/strollers

Nursing stool

Infant activity gym

WORST THINGS TO BORROW OR INHERIT

1. Car Seat
2. Crib

3. Crib Mattress
4. Breast Pump
5. Nursing Bra
6. Infant Toys
7. Bottles and Nipples
8. Pacifiers
9. Diaper Pail
10. Hygiene Supplies (hairbrush, nail clippers, nasal syringe, etc.)

ITEMS YOU CAN EASILY LIVE WITHOUT

Bottle Warmer
Bottle Sterilizer
After-Bath Kimonos
Hooded Towels
Infant Shoes
Drool Bibs
Playpen
Laundry Hamper
Big, luxurious baby carriage or pram
Wipe Warmer

ITEMS YOU'RE BETTER OFF WITHOUT

Any clothing that must be dry-cleaned or ironed (unless it's for a very special occasion)
Bath Ring
Walker
Jumper
Bottle Proppers
Car Seat Head Rest
Car Seat Harness Strap Cushions and other car seat accessories

Sleep Positioners
Crib Bumpers
Moses Basket

FAVORITE NOT-SO-OBVIOUS BABY GIFTS

Baby tape player and tapes
Diapering basket: spray bottle, pump-top Thermos, home-made Aqualox, dry wipes
Picture frames with a picture ledge
Book basket—baby's first library
Gymini infant activity gym
Stay-Warm stroller bag
Infant car seat cover-up
Halo infant sleep sack
Radio Flyer walker wagon: Great for toy storage early on; perfect push toy for rookie walkers. Some specialty stores will personalize them for you.
Waterproof blanket or play mat

Appendix

Part 1: Master Shopping Lists

Optional items

CAR SEATS

Rear-facing infant-only car seat with 3- or 5-point harness, built-in angle adjuster, and detachable base

* Infant car seat coverup—must be designed to fit over seat; do not use any style that must be threaded onto the car seat straps or that lines the seating area of the car seat itself.

Convertible car seat with 5-point harness and 30-pound minimum rear-facing capacity (purchase later, when baby is close to outgrowing infant-only car seat; use the convertible rear facing to the maximum allowable weight or height limit of the seat)

WHEELS

Stroller with full-recline seat and/or Carriage and/or stroller

* Snap-N-Go car seat stroller frame

*Sport-utility stroller

Rain shield

* Under stroller basket (if stroller does not come with one)

* Net stroller bag (to hang off handles—do not overfill)

* Stay-warm stroller bag

* Head and body support pad

* Bug netting

HOLDERS AND CARRIERS

Front carrier or sling

Bouncy seat

Portable play yard (with bassinet attachment if using as a first sleeping spot for baby)

Infant activity gym

High chair (as mentioned in feeding section)

Booster seat for feeding

*Battery-operated baby swing

*Stationary exerciser

*Baby backpack (purchase later, when baby can hold head upright)

BREAST FEEDING

1–2 good books about breastfeeding

2 nursing bras (for starters)

Nursing pillow

Glider and nursing stool (as mentioned in nursery furniture section)

Breast pump (research ahead of time; purchase after baby arrives)

1 tube hospital-grade lanolin

1 box of disposable nursing pads

Four 4-ounce plastic bottles

2 silicone newborn-size (slow-flow) nipples

4–6 single-serving-size cans or bottles of premixed formula or 1 box of single-serving powder sleeves

* Breast milk storage bags

* Breast shells

BOTTLE-FEEDING

6 plastic bottles, small or large size or mix of both

2 silicone, newborn-size (slow-flow) nipples

Bottle brush

*Drying rack

*Dishwasher accessories basket

Dry formula only:

*Dry formula dispenser

*Covered pitcher

*Small thermos

Formula to get started (ask pediatrician for suggested amounts)

Feeding—Later On

High chair (as mentioned in carriers and holders section)

Booster seat for feeding (as mentioned in carriers and holders section)

*Baby food mill

CLOTHING, LINENS, BEDDING

4 side-snap undershirts

8 snap-crotch undershirts (all short-sleeved, or in winter, buy 6 short- and 2 long-sleeved)

2 sleep gowns with elasticized bottoms

8 polyester or cotton stretchies (one-piece sleep/play outfits)

1–2 sleep sacks (for colder months)

4 pairs of socks

4 cloth bibs

2 lightweight caps

2–3 outdoor hats (soft, cozy, snug to head for winter babies; sun hat with flaps for summer babies)

1 fleece snowsuit

Going home outfit

3 receiving blankets

6 baby washcloths

2 hooded or standard towels

12 prefolded cloth diapers

3 fitted changing-pad covers (or more, depending upon how many changing pads you will have)

3 fitted crib sheets

* 2 waterproof lap pads

* 2 fitted bassinet sheets (if you will be using a bassinet)

* 2 fitted sheets for portable play yard, if not included with play yard

NURSERY FURNITURE AND PARAPHERNALIA

Crib

Crib mattress

*Crib skirt

*Bassinet or * co-sleeper or portable play yard with bassinet insert (if baby will not be sleeping in the big crib for starters)

Dresser

Changing table or adequate changing surface

Glider

Nursing stool

Bookshelf

Toy storage baskets or bins

Diaper pail

Trash basket

Laundry basket or hamper

Lamp

CD/tape player

Baby monitor

Window shade

* Ceiling fan

* Dimmer switch for overhead light

DIAPERING ACCESSORIES

Diaper bag

1 or more contoured changing pads

Diaper pail (as mentioned in above nursery list)

Diaper supply caddy

Pump top or regular thermos

Small, empty spray bottle

BATH, HEALTH, AND HYGIENE ESSENTIALS

Baby bathtub

Mesh toy bag with suction cups

Towels, washcloths (as mentioned in clothing, linens, bedding section)

Diapering Supplies

2 tubs of premoistened baby wipes

2 tubes diaper balm

1 bottle regular-strength Maalox

* Dry wipes, such as Chix

If using disposable diapers:

100 newborn-size disposable diapers + 100 size 1; or 200 size 1, if newborn size isn't available

If using cloth diaper service:

4–6 diaper covers (for starters)

30–40 size 1 disposable diapers

Grooming

Firm, nylon-bristled baby hairbrush

Baby manicure set (infant-size clippers, safety scissors, mini emery boards)

Cotton (or pseudo cotton) balls

Cotton swabs

Hair- and Skincare

Head-to-toe baby bath soap

1 large tube Aquaphor

Mild moisturizer (Cetafil is excellent)

* Cold-pressed sweet almond massage oil

Medicine Chest

Rectal thermometer

Nasal syringe

Cool-mist humidifier

2 silicone pacifiers

2 ice packs

Sterile gauze

1 tweezer

2 bottles infant-strength acetaminophen

2 bottles infant-strength ibuprofen

1 tube teething gel

1 bottle infant-strength simethicone drops

1 bottle saline nose drops

2 bottles syrup of ipecac

1 bag activated charcoal

1 tube antibiotic ointment

1 tube .05% hydrocortisone ointment or cream

1 tub or tube of petroleum jelly

1 bottle electrolyte rehydration solution (clear, not colored)

1 calibrated medicine dropper

TOYS

Books

Rattle

Shatterproof infant mirror

Busy box

Baby tape player and tapes

Ball (once baby sits up)

Push toy (early walking)

SAFETY AND BABYPROOFING

Infant car seat (as mentioned in car seat section)

Baby monitor (as mentioned in nursery section)

Gates (if using at top of stairs, buy gates designed specifically for this purpose)

Outlet plugs or covers

Cabinet latches

Drawer latches

Furniture anchors

* Coffee table bumper or corner guards

* Fireplace bumper

FOR THE HOUSE

The Family File:

File cabinet

Hanging folders

Manila folders

Labels

Small spiral notebook

Sharpie permanent ink markers

Kitchen

Paper plates and plastic utensils

Lidded commuter cups

Water bottles

Shelf-stable milk

Frozen meals

Canned soups

Dried and frozen pasta

Parmesan cheese

Canned tuna

Bread (keep in freezer)

Peanut butter

Jelly/jam

Flour tortillas

Decaf coffees and teas

Around the House

Clear plastic shower curtain

Cordless phone with headset

Dustbusters

Pump-top soaps for every sink

2 big boxes baby laundry detergent or dye-free, scent-free adult laundry detergent

Bleach

Borax detergent booster (like 20 Mule Power)

1 stain stick or 1 bottle liquid stain treater

Waterproof mattress cover for Mom's bed

FOR MOM

Date book or Palm Pilot

6–8 pairs big, cheap cotton underpants

2 sets of (nursing-friendly, if applicable) pajamas

Robe with pockets

Tucks

Lots of sanitary napkins or adult diapers

Preparation H

Roomy button-down blouses

Loose T-shirts

Unstructured, elastic-waisted pants

Long black, elastic-waisted skirt

Slip-on shoes, like clogs, slides, thongs

Part 2: Great Sources for Stuff and Info

Epinions, *www.epinions.com:* If the Girlfriends haven't mentioned a product you're interested in, see what other parents are saying on this gigantic opinion site. Baby-gear coverage is considerable.

U.S. Consumer Product Safety Commission, *www.cpsc.gov,* 800-638-2772: Source for product safety information; subscribe to their recall alert list, and they'll e-mail you if something is announced.

Consumer Reports, *www. consumerreports.org:* The online extension of the renowned consumer product publication. Some general info is available for free; a reasonable subscription fee allows access to product ratings and reviews.

American Academy of Pediatrics, *www.aap.org,* 847-434-4000: Extensive info and news on child health and safety, including child sleepwear guidelines and a listing of all new car seats sold in the U.S., along with all their specs.

National Safe Kids Campaign *www.safekids.org,* 800-441-1888: Wide ranging site focusing on child safety.

SafteyBeltSafeU.S.A.: *www. carseat.org* **or 800-745-SAFE or 800-747-SANO:** Accurate and diligent coverage of child passenger safety issues, including specific car-seat usage information.

National Highway Traffic Safety Administration, *www. nhtsa.dot.gov,* 888-DASH-2-DOT: Accurate source for car-seat information, as well as general child passenger safety advice.

Car Seat Data, *www.carseatdata. org:* Unofficial child passenger safety technician-run site; keeps an ongoing list of car/car-seat compatabilities.

The Danny Foundation, *www. dannyfoundation.org,* 800-83-DANNY: Great source for crib safety info.

SIDS Alliance, *www.sidsalliance. org,* 800-221-7437: Promotes medical research and public education about Sudden Infant Death Syndrome.

La Leche League International, *www.lalecheleague.org,* 847-519-7730: Definitive, albeit opinionated, source for breastfeeding info.

International Lactation Consultant Association, *www.ilca.org:* **919-787-5181,** For assistance finding a certified lactation consultant in your area.

International Association for Child Safety, *www.iafcs.org:* **888-677-IACS,** For the name of a childproofing specialist in your area.

The Twins and Supertwins List, *www.twinslist.org:* Terrific site busting with info and advice from parents of multiples.

ON-LINE RETAILERS, DISCOUNTERS, ETC.

Ebay, *www.ebay.com:* Don't assume this auction site is a place for secondhand stuff and offbeat collectibles. Retailers and surplus houses unload overstocks of brand-spankin'-new baby products at amazing prices here. This includes names like Peg Perego and other specialty brands that are traditionally unavailable at discount.

Babystyle, *www.babystyle.com:* Even if you don't buy anything, this site will give you an idea of what's in style and what type of speciality items are hot. For babes, moms-to-be, and new moms.

Babycenter, *www.babycenter.com:* Good, general articles for new and expectant parents; e-mails personalized to your baby's age; and a solid store with helpful consumer reviews.

Pallets, *www.kidsurplus.com:* Fabulously priced overstocks and seconds from name-brand giants, slyly referred to as The Zap, Lamb's End, Old Gravy—you get the idea. Great deals on layettewear, gear, and gifts.

Strollers4Less.com, *www.strollers4less.com:* Competitive prices for wide range of strollers.

The Preemie Store, *www.preemie.com*, **800-676-8469** Specialty products for premature babies.

NATIONAL RETAILERS, WHOLESALE HOUSES

Babies 'Я' Us, *www.babiesrus.com*, **888-BABYRUS:** Good for shopping and general research; solid on-line registry.

Burlington Coat Factory's Baby Depot, *www.coat.com*, **800-444-COAT:** Web site offers shopping and general info about this baby superstore.

Costco, *www.costco.com:* On-line shopping and info about the national warehouse club.

BJ's Wholesale: *www.bjs.com:* info only, no Internet shopping.

Sam's Club, *www.samsclub.com:* on-line shopping and info about the wholesale club

IKEA, *www.ikea.com:* Location info, virtual catalog, and limited on-line shopping available from the web site of this international furnishing and accessory chain.

babyGap, *www.babygap.com*: Easy Internet shopping for baby and preemie garb à la Gap.

CATALOG/INTERNET RETAILERS

Hanna Andersson, *www.hannaandersson.com,* **800-222-0544:** Shop on-line or call for a catalog. Gorgeous, colorful all-cotton clothes for babies and kids. There's also some stuff for Mom. Prices are sorta steep, but the quality is excellent and sales are frequent.

The Wooden Soldier, **603-356-7041:** Call for a catalog if you must get your hands on a christening gown or some other type of incredibly frilly, fancy outfit for your child.

The Right Start, *www.rightstart.com,* **800-548-8531:** On-line,

catalog, or brick-and-mortar shopping for a wide range of baby specialty products and gear.

One Step Ahead, *www.onestepahead.com,* **800-274-8440.** Wide range of baby specialty products. Shop on-line or call for a catalog.

Perfectly Safe, *www.perfectlysafe.com,* **800-898-3696:** Catalog and Web site selling child safety related products. Many are good—but not all are recommended by safety experts and the medical community. Consult the sections in this book on car seats, crib safety, and Sudden Infant Death Syndrome before buying any products related to these issues.

Lilly's Kids, *www.lillianvernon.com,* **800-545-5426:** An offshoot of the Lillian Vernon catalog selling affordable kidswear, toys, personalized gifts, and generally fun stuff you might not run into elsewhere. Quality varies. Shop on-line or call for a catalog.

Constructive Playthings, *www.constplay.com,* **800-448-7830:** Good selection of toys that encourage creativity and open-ended play. Shop, check out store locations on-line, or call for a catalog.

Pottery Barn Kids, *www. potterybarnkids.com*, **800-993-4923:** Stylish furniture, bedding, and design accessories for babies and children.

Lands' End Kids, *www.landsend. com*, **800-963-4816:** Excellent for sleepwear, sportswear, and outerwear source for kids age newborn on up. Lands' End also makes sturdy, functional diaper bags. Shop on-line or call for a catalog.

L.L. Bean Kids, *www.llbean.com*, **800-441-5713:** Well-made sports and outerwear for children; good selection of outerwear, footwear, and sleepwear for babes.

Patagonia Kids, *www.patagonia .com*, **800-638-6464:** Sturdy, but somewhat pricey, selection of outerwear and rugged wear for babies and children.

The Land of Nod, *www.landof nod.com*, **800-933-9904:** Nifty but pricey furniture, bedding, and accessories for children's rooms. Call for a catalog.

Seventh Generation, *www. seventhgen.com*, **802-658-3773** Web site and catalog selling all kinds of biodegradable and earth-friendly stuff for baby and home.

Hold Everything, *www. williams-sonomainc.com*, **800-421-2264:** Containers so nice, they blend right in with the furniture. Not cheap, but pretty.

Container Store, *www. containerstore.com*, **800-733-3532:** Solid, no-nonsense stuff to help you get organized.

The Company Store, *www. thecompanystore.com*, **800-323-8000.** Colorful, high-quality bedding and accessories for babies and kids.

Garnet Hill, *www.garnethill.com*, **800-870-3513:** Gorgeous, natural-fiber clothes, loungewear, sleepwear, maternity clothes, bedding, and more. A particularly great source for comfy yet stylish postpartum duds.

Campmor, *www.campmor.com*, **888-CAMPMOR:** All kinds of outdoor equipment for grown-ups, kids, and babes—at discount prices.

Ofoto, *www.ofoto.com*, **510-229-1200:** On-line photo service that can turn digital and film photography into just about anything—including beautiful baby announcements.

Part 3: What You Absolutely Must Know About Using Car Seats Correctly

Here's what you absolutely must know about buying and using car sets.

1. There is no "safest seat." All new car seats sold in the United States meet government crash-test standards if they are installed and used correctly. *What matters most is that the car seat fits your child and is easy to use and install correctly.*

2. Not every car seat is compatible with every car. Some child restraints have a wide base that just won't fit in the narrow center seat of some cars. Some rear-facing car seats cannot be used in many subcompact cars because their tall backs conflict with the seat in front of them. Even if you are using the LATCH system, you simply cannot be certain that you have purchased an appropriate seat unless you or ideally a CPS technician has actually tried to install it in your vehicle.

3. The rear center seat is the safest spot for a car seat. If the design of your car or other factors prohibit you from installing your child restraint there, either rear window seat is acceptable.

4. A car seat should never go in front of an air bag. If your car does not have a backseat and you cannot afford to buy one that does, a child restraint may be put in the front seat but ONLY if there is no air bag or if the air bags have been professionally deactivated. Failing to do so, especially if your child is seated rear facing (which should never, ever be done), can have deadly results.

5. Children should stay rear facing for as long as possible. The American Academy of Pediatrics' recommendation that children stay rear facing until they are at least **one year and 20 pounds is an absolute bare minimum.** By providing support for a baby's big head and immature neck bones, rear-facing seats significantly reduce their risk of spinal-cord injury, brain damage, and death. When your baby outgrows her infant-only seat, she should be moved to a convertible and kept rear facing to the maximum rear-facing weight or height capacity of the car seat. Under no circumstances should any child under one year of age—regardless of his weight—be turned to face forward.

6. A properly installed car seat should not move more than one inch in any direction. For tips on how to achieve this elusive goal if you are not using LATCH, see "Happiness is a Tight Seat" in this appendix.

7. The car seat harness should be snug to your child. Avoid dressing your child in a big bulky snowsuit or coat—it can make it seem that the harness is tight when it really is not. Opt instead for something like polar fleece and lay a blanket or other warm garments over the harness. Remember, too, that a harness is only fully effective if its straps are kept untwisted and the harness clip (if there is one) is kept at your child's armpit level.

8. Threading harness straps through the incorrect slots can be deadly. When you turn a convertible car seat to face forward, *don't assume that the harness should be threaded through the slots that are nearest your child's shoulders.* The fact is that only the top harness slots in most convertible car seats are reinforced and are thus strong enough to withstand the thrust of a forward-facing child's entire body weight in the event of a severe front-end collision. A harness threaded in an unreinforced slot can literally rip through the back of the car seat and allow your child to be ejected. Check your car-seat manual carefully.

9. It is never okay to take your baby out of her car seat if your car is on the road. Not to soothe him if he's fussy. Not to nurse him. Not if it's a short ride. Not if you're stuck in traffic. You never know when you will be in a collision. You never know when a jolt might deploy your air bag. Mothers have lost their children in just these circumstances. Make this promise to yourself and to your baby. And chew on this last thought: If someone were to tell you that this was the day you were going to be in a collision, which way would you seat your child? How much time would you take to adjust his harness? Would you take him out of his seat even for a second? You should get into your car with that attitude every day.

Part 4: Happiness Is a Tight Seat

Whether or not your car is LATCH-equipped, the following tips should help you install your car seat correctly.

BUY THE RIGHT SEAT FOR YOUR CAR.
Some car seats, no matter how highly rated or praised they may be, just aren't compatible with some cars. To get an idea of what models might be appropriate for your vehicle, log on to *carseatdata.org*, an unofficial, technician-run site that keeps a list of car/car-seat compatabilities. Then "try before you buy" (or at least before you file that receipt)—and only shop where it's easy to make a return.

READ YOUR CAR-SEAT INSTRUCTIONS.
It sounds obvious. But the fact is parents turn to the car-seat manual as a last resort, when it should be the very first thing they do. And don't just skim that dry, technical text—read it line by line, because it includes some not-so-obvious information about your specific car seat that can directly impact your child's safety. Pay equal attention to the car-seat section of your vehicle manual—

a vital resource most parents completely overlook. If you do not have the manual for the car seat or vehicle, contact the manufacturer and they will send one.

GET THE ANGLE.
This part is sort of technical, but hang in there. All car seats are designed so that when their base is horizontal to the ground, the seat itself will hold a child at the angle that is deemed safest by the manufacturer. In the rear-facing position, this angle is usually between 30 and 45 degrees. The problem is, most vehicle seats are slanted downward to some extent. Several car seats now come with an adjustable base that can be raised to help compensate for this tilt. But many parents still end up sticking something under the car seat base in order to make it level. Instead of using a rolled up towel, as some car-seat manuals recommend, technicians work with—would you believe—pool noodles, those long, spongy water toys. If your vehicle seat is very slanted, you can bundle and duct-tape together up to three equal lengths of pool noodle. When it's time to

turn your child forward facing (one year and 20 pounds at the absolute minimum, preferably longer), check that car-seat manual again. Among other things, it will tell you how to switch the base adjustment mechanism so your child will sit upright and the car seat will fit tighter in the forward-facing position. *Do not use pool noodles or anything else to prop the car seat when it is forward facing. It is unnecessary and manufacturers have not officially done crash testing to assure that it is safe.*

IF YOU ARE NOT USING LATCH, KNOW THY SEAT BELTS.

Simply put, when you use a seat belt to install a car seat, that seat belt must somehow, in some way, be prevented from letting out slack. Otherwise, your car seat will end up swimming around the backseat of your car no matter what heroic efforts you make. As luck would have it, not all vehicle belt systems "lock" the same way. The easiest way to find out what you have on your hands, is to consult that oh-so-handy vehicle manual and proceed as instructed. Food for thought: If your seat-belt system requires the use of a separate locking clip, consider buying a convertible car seat that comes

with this feature built in when your child grows out of his infant-only seat (only Britax currently offers this). It's a more expensive route, but it's far easier and less frustrating than trying to use the separate metal locking clip that comes with other seats.

MAKE IT TIGHT.

Now, if you are not using LATCH, it's time to get this puppy in tight—which means the car seat should move no more than one inch in any direction when you push and pull it forcefully at the point where the vehicle belt passes through the seat. Fat chance, you say? First, follow all directions to a T. If the seat still wiggles, lean even harder into the seat while installing it—we actually get on top of it and push our backs into the top of the car for extra leverage—then get rid of any slack. Placing a square of spongy shelf liner under the car seat can also help reduce slipping and sliding significantly (especially in cars with slick leather or fabric seats). Other than the materials suggested above, avoid using anything else, even store-bought gadgets, that may seem to help tighten the fit. There are no government standards set for the use of any after-market products with car seats—regardless of what the packaging might imply. As a result, there's no way to tell how a product will perform in a crash.

PUT OUTERWEAR ON TOP.

During a collision, everything between a car seat's harness straps and the back of the car seat becomes compressed—including the coat and clothing your child is wearing. As a result, a harness that seemed tight can become loose, making it possible for your child to actually be ejected from the seat. To keep your child's harness snug, dress your child with as little bulk as possible and be sure to drape blankets and anything else over, instead of under, the harness straps. The point is to make the harness tight to the child, not to his jacket. Those fleece "bubbles" designed for rear-facing infant-only seats are an excellent option. Just be sure the one you buy fits over and around the outside of the seat and does not interfere in any way with the harness.

USE THAT TETHER.

Top tethers now come with every new car seat that can be used in a forward-facing position. And it's well worth using yours when it's time to turn your child around. By anchoring the top of a forward-facing car seat to a vehicle's tether anchor, a top tether dramatically reduces how far a child's head can be thrust forward during a collision. An added bonus: A tether will also provide better overall stability for the seat. Your vehicle manual will tell you where the tether anchor is located in your car; if you have an older model, the manual will tell you if and where an anchor can be installed. Ford, DaimlerChrysler, and GM retrofit older vehicles free of charge.

SCHEDULE A CHECKUP.

Now that you've got all the inside tips, give installation a go. Then pay a visit to a certified CPS technician so we can give your work the once-over. And provide you with some much deserved kudos. If all of this simply leaves your head spinning, skip the above antics and just come and see us. You can even come straight from the superstore with your car seat still in the box. Techs will figure out if and how the seat fits your vehicle and your child, check to make sure it's not recalled, and most important—show you how to install it all by yourself. The National Highway Traffic Safety Administration Web site (*nhtsa.dot.gov*) maintains a list of car-seat checkup events, as well as a directory of institutions and individuals qualified to provide free child passenger safety checkups. You can also contact the following organizations directly: DaimlerChrysler Fit for Kid: 877-FIT-4-AKID; *www.fitforakid.org;*

National SAFE KIDS Campaign: 800-441-1888; *www.safekids.org;* International Association of Chiefs of Police: 1-800-THE-IACP; Boost America!: 866-BOOST-KID; *www.boostamerica.org*

April/May 2002, Weider Publications, Inc. Reprinted with permission.

Index

Index

Index

Index

Index

Index

About the Authors

Vicki Iovine, a mother of four, lives with her family in southern California. She is also the author of *The Girlfriends' Guide to Pregnancy, The Girlfriends' Guide to Surviving the First Year of Motherhood, The Girlfriends' Guide to Toddlers, The Girlfriends' Guide to Getting Your Groove Back,* and *The Girlfriends' Guide to Parties and Playdates.* Visit Vicki Iovine on-line at *www.girlfriendsguide.com.*

Peg Rosen writes about health and family for numerous parenting and women's service publications. She has been on the staff of *Bride's* magazine and most recently *Child*, where she was a senior editor in charge of new products, prenatal health, and early childhood development. A Certified Child Passenger Safety Technician, Ms. Rosen writes and lectures often to parents about car seat safety. She lives and works in Montclair, New Jersey, with her husband, Paul Freundlich, and sons, Ben and Noah.